Lessons from a Child

On the Teaching and Learning of Writing

LUCY McCORMICK CALKINS

Teachers College, Columbia University

Portsmouth
Heinemann Educational Books
London • Melbourne

Heinemann Educational Books
70 Court Street, Portsmouth, New Hampshire 03801
22 Bedford Square, London WCIB 3HH

EDINBURGH   MELBOURNE   AUCKLAND
HONG KONG   SINGAPORE   KUALA LUMPUR   NEW DELHI
IBADAN   NAIROBI   JOHANNESBURG
KINGSTON   PORT OF SPAIN

First published 1983

Reprinted 1984 (twice)

Library of Congress Cataloging in Publication Data

Calkins, Lucy McCormick.
  Lessons from a child.

  Bibliography: p.
  1. English language—Composition and exercises.
I. Title.
LB1576.C312   1983   372.8'74   83-8599
ISBN 0-435-08206-X

Cover photograph and photographs for parts I and II by Larry Kennedy

Cover design by Ryan Cooper

Printed in the United States of America

Contents

Acknowledgements   v

I A writing workshop begins

1. A research project, a classroom, a child   3
2. Re-Vision   9
3. A partnership forms   20
4. Topics which tap the energy to write   24
5. The structure of a writing workshop   30
6. Editing: last but not least   33
7. The teacher's role   37

II One child's growth in writing

8. First lessons   43
9. Revision?   49
10. From writer to reader: Susie develops an
    executive function   55
11. Sequences in Susie's writing development   62
12. The life-story of one text   68
13. Between the lines: Susie's process becomes
    internalized   76
14. Longer stories and bigger revisions   89

III The writing classroom: a context for growth

15. When teachers collaborate: new ideas   105
16. Twenty six teachers in this classroom   114
17. Peer conferences thread through the writing
    process   117
18. Teaching children to teach each other   125
19. Teaching by example   131
20. When children conference with themselves   138
21. Concept development   142
22. Reading-writing connections   152
23. Reading, writing and a glacier report   160
24. Lessons from children   172

Bibliography   177
Index   179

Dedicated to my first and finest teachers

Evan and Virginia Calkins

*and to the person who showed me
how to learn from children*

Donald Graves

Acknowledgements

At its heart, *Lessons from a Child* is autobiographical. Although it is a research chronicle, it is also a personal narrative. It has grown not only from two years of research and three years of drafting and revision, but also from thirty-one years of teaching and learning in classrooms.

Those classrooms were not always contained within the walls of school buildings. Some of my most important lessons about education were learned during my own childhood. There were nine children in our family: we each had projects, and through them we each learned that the line between work and play is a thin one. Until I was eight, I had a chicken flock of my own and sold eggs around the neighborhood. Then for a while it was the nearby swamp which caught my fancy and so every spring the bathtubs in our large brick farmhouse held pollywogs and lettuce leaves. Later, as an adolescent, I gathered friends together on weekends and we wrote plays and marionette shows under the pine trees that lined our lawn. My parents not only encouraged our projects—they had their own, teaching by example as well as by encouragement. How grateful I am for those early classrooms.

It was as an undergraduate at Williams College that I first read Dewey, Tillich, Piaget, Tolstoy, Erikson and others and began to see teaching as a way to make meaning in my own life while helping others do the same. "We are the teaching species," Erikson wrote. "Human beings need to teach, not only for the sake of those who need to be taught but for the fulfullment of our identities, and because facts are kept alive by being told, truths by being professed."

Thankfully, my first teaching experiences were in an urban high school where attendance averaged 60% and students weren't afraid to ask hard questions. "Why am I supposed to learn about Eygpt?" they'd ask. "This is crazy stuff. Why are we doing this? So what?" When my year was over, I asked myself the same questions. "Why am I doing this? So what?"

In search of a vision, I began teaching first in Oxfordshire, England and then in an alternative public school in Middlefield, Connecticut. Those readers who visited the British Primary

Schools at their best will recognize ways in which their emphasis on collaborative learning, student initiative and craftsmanship have been re-discovered and extended within the context of the writing workshop. I agree with the great British educator, Charity James, who urges us to remember the roots of our innovations:

> We are apt to think of our innovations as a new growth of the human spirit, which indeed they are, but this aspect in isolation can make the whole work seem too exciting, too perishable, for its own good. We must see ourselves also in this period as holding the line, as helping to maintain, through our new relationships with students and our new hopes for their learning, an older humanism which the march of matter, the parade of power, would otherwise destroy.

From my colleagues in each of these teaching settings, I learned what I could never have learned from graduate courses. I'm particularly grateful to Peggy Stevens, Joy Mermin, Bud Church, Sue Devokaitis and to a student of mine—Rebecca Lavine. Some of my readers will remember from my earlier publications a poem Rebecca wrote when she was eight:

I climbed the snowy boulder,
My throne.
I grabbed an ice-covered stick,
My staff.
Icey snow sprinkled in my face,
My veil.
"Rebecca, come help shovel."
I clambored off the snow,
Me again.

This poem helped me see how powerful it can be when children put into print their view of the world: thank you, Rebecca.

It was during those years as a teacher that I first began to work with Pulitzer Prize winning writer, Donald M. Murray. Although the only writing I'd done until then were papers for school, Murray agreed to work with my writing. Every six weeks, I'd take a day off from school and make the three hour drive to the University of New Hampshire where Murray would confer with me for thirty minutes and then I'd turn around and make the three hour drive back to Connecticut. Now, years later, I try to recapture the secret of Murray's teaching. Whatever happened during those conferences, it not only made the trip worthwhile, it also transformed my writing and teaching of writing. It would be impossible to give adequate credit to Murray for all I've learned from him—even the words *rehearsal, drafting, revision,* and *editing* are words he selected. Only Susie herself has had an equal impact on this book.

Lessons from a Child begins at this point in my life-line: a phone call from Donald Graves, the decision to leave teaching for full-time research and writing; these events are contained within the text. The characters in this next drama are there too: the teachers from Atkinson Elementary School, especially Carolyn Currier, Pat Howard and Mary Ellen Giacobbe; the principal, Jean Robbins; my research colleague, Susan Sowers; our secretary, Lois Cyr; our funding agency, The National Institute of Education; and of course, the children . . . Birger, Craig, Diane, Amy, Susie and so many others.

All these people played a part in the research project but it was Donald Graves who truly gave me the gift of those years, those lessons. Graves showed me that beneath every research project there are human beings with stories to tell. "Every child has a story to tell," he often said, quoting Harold Rosen. "The question is, will they tell it to us?"

The answer was yes. Children, teachers, principals told us their stories because Graves showed us how to listen, how to see the significance in what others might think was ordinary.

Graves helped me see that the children had stories to tell—but it has been the teachers, graduate students and colleagues with whom I've worked since the study who've helped me realize that I, too, have a story to tell. In some ways, *Lessons from a Child* is part of an oral tradition. In summer institutes, graduate courses and workshops, I've shared and developed the ideas embedded in this book. In each of these contexts, students and colleagues have helped me explore the nooks and crannies of these ideas. I'm grateful to all of these people, but especially to Marilyn Boutwell, Hindy List and Shelley Harwayne.

Many teachers have asked hard questions and nudged me to make new connections, but teachers from the New York City public schools have gone a step farther and asked me into their classrooms. And so, three years ago I began conducting writing workshops in classrooms which hold 35 children, often speaking a total of ten different native languages. I went into the classrooms to demonstrate teaching methods . . . and soon found that once again, teachers and I were learning from children. Next year we will be working in eight districts in New York City . . . and I can't help but think that the lessons learned in a white clapboard schoolhouse in rural New Hampshire have shown amazing universality.

There are many others to thank. Gordon Pradl, Harold Vine and Bernice Cullinan advised me on an early version of the book, and helped me see the research within a broader context. Frank Smith reviewed yet another draft. He asked hard and insightful questions and gave me the energy to answer them. My editor, Philippa Stratton, has guided the final revisions and editing.

Now that the book is finished, Mary Ellen Giacobbe's phone bill will plummet for she has responded to each of its many drafts. "The mark of a good responder," Murray once said, "is that writers leave, wanting to write." By cheering me on, delighting in each breakthrough and sensing when to give feedback and when to listen, Mary Ellen Giacobbe has done just that for me.

Whereas Mary Ellen played this role through long distance phone calls, my husband, John Skorpen, played it through the ins and outs of everyday life. "Focus on the writer and the writing will take care of itself," Graves has often said, and this has been my husband's philosophy as well. John has listened not only *to* my writing but also *through* it, hearing when I need encouragement and when I need perspective. He has shared not only the emerging content of the book—the characters from it have become part of our life together—but also he has shared the seasons of my involvement.

And last of all, I'm grateful to Susie . . . but her contribution is well documented in the pages that follow.

I.

A writing workshop begins

1. A research project, a classroom, a child

Shafts of June sunlight angled into the small New Hampshire classroom, breathing a contemporary openness into the room. There was a sense of anticipation in the classroom, as if textbooks suddenly felt lighter and gradebooks could be put aside. But for me, the approach of summer carried a bittersweet sadness, for it meant the close of our research project.

As I scanned the familiar classroom, my eyes lingered on each youngster's face. In every nook and cranny, young writers were at work. Some worked together, conferring with each other as they wrote. Others worked alone.

I smiled at the sight of tow-headed Birger, for despite the summer warmth, his ever-present Norwegian sweater hung on the back of his chair. Birger's writing was draped over three desks—a patchwork of paragraphs and sentences welded together with scotch tape and staples. He looked up and our eyes met. Sensing my interest, Birger launched into an explanation. "I kept on reading my squirrel report over," he said, "and then I'd think if I needed to put more in, or change things, or add excitement." He pointed to a flap hanging from his scroll-like paper. "See, this is draft eight, I stapled it right on top." From the far end of the classroom, the teacher reminded her class it was time to put away the writing and come to a class meeting. Soon a circle of twenty-six fourth graders sat waiting to help each other with work in progress.

It was at that moment that the classroom door opened and the visitor slipped into the room. I'd been expecting him all morning—he was one of a stream of visitors from this country and abroad who wanted to see if the research reports were true. Could children really do so much as writers?

The teacher called on Susie. I was glad, for the soft-spoken, earnest youngster had been the focus of my research for two years. Susie blushed but her eyes smiled. It was this combination of forces—of restraint and eagerness, of shyness and laughter—which had been part of Susie and of her writing ever since I began my case study of her.

As her classmates settled into their cross-legged positions on the floor, Susie glanced down at her papers. From across the circle, her best friend Diane stage-whispered "Hey, Sus, tell about the first draft."

Susie nodded. "When I read over my first draft of 'At the Beach,' I thought 'How did it feel?' 'What was it like?' 'What was I thinking when I stood on the beach?'" She glanced across the circle to where her friend Diane sat, then continued. "I realized probably my whole first draft was like that—blah. So I wrote a whole new draft." Susie looked at her teacher as if to ask whether she should read the improved version.

"Why don't you read the beginning of each draft so we can hear your revisions," her teacher suggested. The children pulled closer as Susie began to read.

Draft 1
I was at a beach in Florida. I pressed my toes into the hot sand. I saw my sister jumping out in the waves with my Aunt. She was jumping around as the waves hit her, she was out deep . . . I wanted to go and play in the big waves but I was nervous to.

Draft 2
I pressed my toes into the hot sand. I wiggled them around. The gritty sand felt good on my sunburnt toes. I looked out over the ocean. My sister was out deep, jumping over waves with my Aunt. Sometimes the waves got too big and they would knock her over, then my Aunt would pull her up and she'd be dripping wet and they'd start laughing. My shoulders were hot from the burning sun. I would have loved to be out there in the waves but I was too scared.

The visitor's pleased eyes met mine. He whispered, "I got here just in time."

I thought of the changes in Susie's writing and in her classrooms since I'd entered her world two years earlier. Our visitor hadn't seen the changing interactions between Susie, her teachers and her classmates, or the accompanying changes in her writing strategies. Two years ago, Susie and most of her classmates attended more to the conventions of language than to the content. At the start of third grade, Susie wrote rarely. When she did, it was on assigned topics and she wrote one draft only. If she made revisions, they centered on spelling and punctuation rather than on information, tone and voice. Over the course of third and fourth grade, Susie and her classmates had developed as writers, gaining experience in the craft of writing. Now many of them were relentless revisers. They'd learned to wrestle for the words to convey memories, images and information. They'd written personal narratives, content area reports, letters, stories and poems.

Our visitor had seen the product but he'd missed out on the process. He'd missed the story of Susie's growth in writing, and of how writing was taught and learned in her classrooms. "I guess we see it differently," I said to him. "I'd say you got here just too late."

Lessons from a Child is the story of what I learned because I wasn't too late. Through a grant from the National Institute of Education, I documented the day-to-day changes in Susie's writing and in her classrooms during her third and fourth grade years. With clipboard in hand, I participated in and followed Susie's—and her classmates'—growth in writing.

This is the first study of its kind. A great many researchers have examined written products, dividing them into categories and levels. But rarely in the research findings do we catch a glimpse of a youngster, bending over her paper, surrounded by the sounds of pencils being sharpened, of stories being shared. And nowhere in the research do we find a record of daily changes in a youngster's writing process. Nowhere do we watch as a child graduates from a thick red pencil to a thin yellow one, from writing one draft to shuttling between many. Why haven't more researchers thought to pull their chairs alongside youngsters' desks and watch what the youngsters do during writing? The method seems so obvious, so logical. It's hard to imagine why no one thought of it before.

Yet I, too, did not see the obvious. It was Donald Graves who had the vision to conceive of this study. I was a classroom teacher at the time, working in an alternative public school and writing about my work. My articles were just beginning to appear in *Language Arts* and in *Learning Magazine*. Being published was exciting, but what was more important was that writing had turned my teaching into learning, propelling me into a position of actively constructing meanings out of my teaching. Yet like so many teachers, although I observed children, developed hunches, and gathered information, I saw myself as neither a creator nor a consumer of research. The specialized vocabulary and statistical framework associated with research had built a mystique around it and it never would have occurred to me that my records were data, that I was a researcher.

In fact, I was suspicious of research. It seemed so alien to classrooms and children. My first thought when Graves asked me to come to the University of New Hampshire as a full-time researcher was, "Why should I leave the children for reams of charts and numbers?" My second thought was, "Why is he asking me, a teacher?"

But I soon found Graves had a different idea of research. Both Graves and his funding source, the National Institute of Education, wanted a research project which bridged theory and practice, a project which would show teachers and children in the context of their classrooms. And they wanted the findings to reach teachers as well as researchers.

And so I moved to an old farmhouse two miles from the University of New Hampshire, and we began the research project, "How Children Change as Writers." Graves had already chosen the public school in Atkinson, New Hampshire as the site for our study. We spent our first day visiting the area. Atkinson is located along the southern border of New Hampshire. Two country roads cross and a village store stands at their intersection. Nearby are two churches, one flanked by a graveyard and the other, by a brick library. Down the road is the white wooden schoolhouse with a flag flying overhead and, beneath the pine trees, a carefully lettered sign which reads:

Atkinson Academy
incorporated 1787
built 1803
the second coeducational school
in America.

There is a classical symmetry to the face of the building, a symmetry which is highlighted by its bell tower. But a closer look reveals that at the back of the school, additions and portable classrooms jut this way and that. Inside the building too, there are signs of the skyrocketing school population, the result of New Hampshire's low tax rates and of Boston's widening belt of influence. Many classrooms are crowded, and every storage closet has long ago been converted into instructional space. It is not a wealthy district. Starting salaries for a teacher are below $10,000, and the per capita expense for each student averages about $1,340. But the school nevertheless had a special aura about it—and I trusted Graves' choice.

The choice was not based on convenience, for Atkinson is almost an hour's drive from the University of New Hampshire. Nor was the choice based on the school's approach to writing. When the study began, children at Atkinson, as in most schools, wrote rarely, and when they did, they wrote for teachers who merely corrected and graded the papers. Graves chose Atkinson because the teachers cared about children. He also chose it because he knew the importance of a strong principal, and Jean Robbins was certainly strong. Robbins was determined to have us at her school. She must have sensed what none of us did at the time: that such a research project would have an immense impact on her school.

Our intention in the study was to build a tentative map of children's growth in writing from first to fourth grade. Joining Graves and me in this effort were research associate Susan Sowers and secretary Lois Cyr. This research team did not assemble en masse alongside Susie's desk, for the case study of Susie was only a part of the larger study involving sixteen children and seven classrooms. Our plan was to follow first graders through second grade, and third graders through fourth grade. Although this book focuses on lessons learned from one child, Susie's story is embedded in the larger research project and in the ebb and flow of life at Atkinson Elementary School.

Susie grew as all children do—all in one piece, with spurts and plateaus, in tears and laughter, and above all, through interactions with friends, teachers, texts, family and with herself. And so *Lessons from a Child* encompasses the full drama of classroom life. Although some may read it for information on specific topics, *Lessons from a Child* is more a tapestry than a textbook. In the book, as in the real-life story, threads interweave, and changes in Susie's writing occur within the context of the changes in her friends, her teachers and her researchers.

Some may ask, "What can the story of one child say about writing development in general?" I could answer by listing commonalities between Susie's growth and her classmates'. I could cite similarities between the children in New Hampshire and the New York City children with whom I now work. But to do these things would be to miss the point. For more than anything, I hope this study highlights the need to learn from other young writers at work in their classrooms. My hope is that through closely observing one child's growth in writing, we'll learn to watch for and to respect each child's growth in writing. My hope is that by understanding the pathways one child has taken in learning to write, we may be able to discern and trust the pathways other children will take. Susie is representative of all children in that she, too, is unique.

As teachers, we have always known that every child's writing development involves the special combination of that youngster's personal style, cognitive development, and writing instruction. Although writing development is talked about "in general," it always happens "in particular." In the end, we always teach unique children: all our students are case-studies.

Or is the reverse true? Is it the children who teach, and we who learn? The irony of this book is that when we regard our students as unique and fascinating, when they become case-study subjects even while they are students, then the children become our teachers, showing us how they learn. I have named this book *Lessons from a Child* because after many drafts, I discovered that it is not the story of a child learning to write. It is the story of a researcher learning to teach.

2. Re-Vision

I left Mrs. Howard's classroom early on my first day as a researcher. Outside, the crispness of that September day only sharpened my disappointment. Partly it had been the crowded classroom, the silent rows of children, their desks piled high with textbooks, workbooks and ditto sheets. The classroom had seemed more like a junior high than a third-grade room. But driving back to our research office at the university, I realized it was more than that. I'd wanted to take over as teacher, to bring parakeets and plants into the room, to push the desks into clusters and to hang bright fabrics over the pale green walls. A new school year had begun and I wasn't sure I liked having a clipboard instead of a classroom.

In fact, I had felt foolish holding that clipboard—like a kid, dressed up in her mother's high heels. I had wondered, "What am I supposed to do? Do I just write stuff down? What do I write?"

I've since learned that this loss of identity is common even for experienced fieldworkers. As Agar writes, "Suddenly you do not know the rules anymore . . . You have no idea what is expected of you" (1980, p. 55). Thankfully I had research colleagues. On my second day as a researcher, Don Graves joined me in Pat Howard's third-grade classroom. The children weren't writing but Graves suggested we stay. I paced up and down the rows. The kids were all copying things out of their math books. I anxiously waited for someone to *do something* so I could gather some data. But no, they just kept on copying out of those math books. I went to the back of the room and leaned against the radiator to wait for some data to appear. Nothing. Finally I signaled to Graves, who'd been scurrying about, and we left.

Before I could let out a quiet groan, Graves burst out with, "What a gold mine! Wasn't it amazing? How'd you suppose that one kid up front could write with a two-inch long pencil? And that guy with the golf ball eraser on the end of his pen. Zowie." In his enthusiasm, Graves didn't notice my silence. He continued, "Wasn't it something the way some kids had desks down around their knees; chairs so high, desks so low. . . . Imagine what that does for penmanship!" he said. "And then those other kids; on

,their low little chairs, reaching up to desks that towered over them . . . "

I had learned a big lesson. The task of case-study research is to make the familiar unfamiliar.

I took the children's writing home with me that night. Ostensibly my task was to sort the papers into categories of less able, average, and above average writers so we could begin selecting our eight third-grade subjects. In reality, I wanted to practice noticing. I wanted to develop the eyes to see.

The writing was a disappointment. The pieces seemed voiceless, lifeless. Even the seven writers I classified as "above average" had written cautious little pieces. Susie's piece, for example, went like this:

> Once there was a clockmaker named Sam. Sam owned a shop on Klicket Street. He lived there with his wife and cat. He made clocks of all kinds. Sam and his wife were very content. Even the cat looked pleased. He got up at 8:00 and washed up and ate at 8:30. He started making clocks at 9:00. He usually went to bed at 10:00. On weekends he worked in the garden. But when he was a little boy he always wanted a dog. . . . It took a while for the dog and cat to get along.[1]

I tried to find interesting features in each story and so I noticed that Susie's piece began with a conventional beginning. I wondered if she'd deliberately tried to answer the "who, what, where, when, why" questions. She had used storybook words such as "content" rather than "happy." Her tale followed two separate themes—their only apparent connection was that both were borrowed from storybooks. The story ended with the dog and cat living happily ever after—an ending which appeared to have been chosen not because it fit the story but because it fit story conventions. In general, it seemed that Susie, like many of her classmates, had written with borrowed words and conventions rather than with images, ideas and memories.

The next day I watched several children as they wrote. One of them happened to be Susie—she was, at the time, just one of many children. Susie toiled to make her margins straight and her letters even, but she did not deliberate over her content or reconsider what she had written. If Susie stood out at all that day, it was because she was amenable to my attention. Her concern with form over content was not unusual, and her writing was fluent but far from exceptional.

---

[1] Spelling and punctuation are corrected unless they are the topic of discussion.

I was spending time in Mrs. Giacobbe's first grade as well as in Mrs. Howard's third grade and I liked it better there. The room emanated a sense of confidence. On the first day of school, Mrs. Giacobbe presented each youngster with a beautiful bound book. "This is for your writing," she said to the five- and six-year-olds. "You can draw and you can write."

Mrs. Giacobbe's confidence was rewarded. The youngsters did not say, "But we can't write." (Research has shown that ninety percent of all children come to school believing they can write and certainly Mrs. Giacobbe's children seemed sure they could put their marks onto the shiny pages of their books.) The children happily trotted back to round tables and, with bright marker pens, began to write. They wrote "as best they could." For several, this meant scribble-writing underneath drawings. But for most of the children, writing meant encoding sounds into words. Although their letters wobbled up and down the page, their voices boomed.

Jose's story read "two people are playing tick-tac-toe":

Five-year-old Chris wrote directions in his book for how to make a robot. These are the first of his thirteen steps, shown in his own spelling:

1. get a hed
2. atuch one liot
3. atach the athr liot
4. Get the boty

His final step was this:

13. Put a sekrt hand in the boty

In the math area, a cluster of children made menus for their make-believe restaurant. They wrote one set of menus in print, the other in what the youngsters called curlicue. When I asked about the difference, Jonathan said, "Simple." Pointing to the curlicue menus, he explained, "These are for grown-ups, the others are for kids."

Even the titles of the children's writing reflected confidence. Imagine a five-year-old writing "How to Make a Robot," or a six-year-old writing "My Recipe Book"! With childlike egocentricity, these children believed they were experts on a whole world of things.

Whereas the older children fretted over how to make their stories "okay" or "right" or "exciting enough," the six-year-olds built their stories much as they built their block constructions. Just as they fearlessly constructed garages, towers, even cities out of a handful of blocks, so, too, they fearlessly wrote letters, signs, newspapers and books out of a handful of consonants.

Whereas the third graders' stories had seemed similar to each other—as if each was from the same mold—the first graders' stories each bore the imprint of the author's personality. Jen's tale is an example; it was named after Woody Owl, a rubber bird she carried about tucked into the waistband of her corduroy trousers.

Me and Woody
by Jen

I like summer. It is fun. With Woody, it is fun. But oh, it is good. Woody catched me and I said, 'Let's ride on my bike.' Honk, honk. Then we played the same thing again.

How different Jen's story is from Susie's rather wooden, cautious tale. In fact, the two youngsters seem to have been engaged in different tasks altogether. In large, splashy letters, Jen has left her mark. Her writing reflects her style, her life-force. As Graves reports, "Jen was saying, 'I am.'"

In neither the content nor the voice of Susie's early third-grade writing was she saying, "I am." Her writing was a display of spelling and penmanship—not her mark on the world. Instead of putting herself on the line, Susie had chosen a safer challenge.

As I looked around the third-grade classroom, there were many examples of children who had learned to take few risks in their writing. Somewhere between first and third grade, the playfulness and personal investment had gone from composition. The safe route was easier, but it didn't tap the children's energy. Melodies do not emerge from finger drills unless the pianist shifts into a listening mode.

I began to call this "the third-grade plateau." Having learned to write adequate conventional pieces, the children's writing development was slowing to a halt. I suspected stories would get longer, more correct and more conventional, and that students would graduate from "Once Upon a Time" to five-paragraph themes. And I envied Don Graves and Susan Sowers whose research focus was on first graders.

From my research pedestal, I was quick to decide that their classroom environment was at the root of Jen's and her class-mates' confidence and willingness to experiment in print, and of Susie's and her classmates' fears of being wrong. Certainly the classrooms were as different as the children in them.

In the first-grade classroom, the teacher had pushed desks into clusters and hung careful signs over each area: *writing, art, math, reading, projects.* Even the hamster's cage bore a label: *Chipper.* Framed pieces of fabric had been hung on the pale green walls and plants lined the window ledge. Children in this room worked with independence. In the writing area, youngsters selected their paper from racks displaying their options: huge sheets of experi-ence chart paper, unlined white paper, lined second-grade paper and blank books of assorted sizes. The children also selected their own topics, and registered their choices on a twelve-foot scroll containing the authors' names and lists of their writing subjects. The children even selected their spellings, sounding out each word as best they could. When they finished, Mrs. Giacobbe listened to the children's stories and helped them expand their content. "Chris," she might say, "I had no idea how to build a robot!" Pulling her chair alongside Chris', she'd continue, "Why don't we read every step over carefully and you can think about each one. Think whether you've told me enough, or if there is more to add." Then the two of them would read the book togeth-er. Only after attending to content would Mrs. Giacobbe notice a child's spelling and punctuation. Even then, she first celebrated what the child *had* done, and only later helped the youngster take the work one step further.

Mrs. Giacobbe's approach to early writing was based on the belief that children can learn to write just as they learn to talk. When a toddler says "ady" instead of Father, we do not worry the child will fixate on bad habits. We are not afraid to let children talk as best they can. We view their errors as closer and closer approx-imations. We delight in whatever the baby *can* do. Mrs. Giacobbe responded similarly to her children's early writing.

Mrs. Howard's classroom was the opposite, and it reminded me of classrooms I'd known as a kid. Other than three windows, the coat-rack (bulging with bright parkas), and a "clean tooth" display on one small bulletin board, the room was lined with chalkboards. These held lists of spelling words for groups A, B and C, a math assignment from the textbook, and directions for each reading group. The desks stood in once-even rows, and if Mrs. Howard left the room, children would dart from one desk to another, depositing messages on carefully folded bits of paper.

When we began the study, Pat Howard promised me that her children would write every day. And so for fifteen minutes, squeezed between reading and snack, she'd present children with topics, pass out paper, and remind her students to watch out for spelling mistakes. Clearly, I decided, it was not from their genes but from their environment that the children (including Susie) had learned to value transcription over composition. I felt certain Pat Howard's teaching methods were the reason why the youngsters regarded composition as an exercise in spelling, penmanship and punctuation.

My intent had been to study development, but by late September I realized I could not overlook the importance of instruction . . . or more specifically, of the teacher, Mrs. Howard. Much of my attention during the early phases of the study turned to the teaching of writing—for I worried that I could not document growth in writing unless the classroom environment allowed that growth to take place. Therefore, in the early section of this book, as in the early section of our study, my focus will be on the classroom environment and on the teaching of writing.

For those first weeks of school, I'd politely, even cautiously circled around the thirty-seven-year-old teacher, hoping, I suppose, I could be invisible. I didn't know what to say to her. Each morning Pat Howard entered the teachers' room with long purposeful strides and, tossing her furry coat onto the couch, she'd sit in her usual place, a tall plastic container of coffee in one hand and children's papers in the other. She'd speak immediately. "Didn't have time to drink my coffee; all that rushing to get Frank and the kids out of the house on time, and that dog wouldn't come in again." Quickly she'd pour coffee out of the container and into her cup, smiling at the others' conversations, her curls bouncing as she laughed a little longer than the others and as she nodded eagerly at their stories. "No! Is that right?" she'd say, participating one hundred percent in the conversations, as she did in everything else. People responded to her attention, and their stories became more animated and longer than they would have been before Pat arrived. When it was Pat's turn to entertain the others, she did this well, regaling them with stories about the dog, and about Amy's and Trevor's escapades. Often in her stories, Pat poked fun at herself, and those tales would end with,

"Frank and the kids could just kill me sometimes." Sometimes one or two children would poke their faces into the teachers' room and beckon to their teacher. Leaving her half-full coffee cup on the shelf, Pat would go to them. We could hear her laughing and saying, "No! Is that right," as she and the children headed off to their classroom.

She was a veteran teacher. Although she wasn't one to talk about her curriculum, people sensed her confidence. I wasn't surprised to learn she was chairman of the math curriculum committee, and served on several other such groups. In fact, I figured Pat was satisfied with everything about her teaching.

For a while, I avoided looking at her so she wouldn't look at me. But her approach to teaching writing troubled me. By mid-September, I sensed that ignoring it was no longer an option. I figured that unless the writing program changed, the "third-grade plateau" might better be called the "third-grade deadend." Should I get involved in instruction? Would that help? What was my role in this classroom to be?

Every participant observer asks these questions and answers them, too, consciously or unconsciously. I wanted my answers to be conscious.

I felt torn. Not by a fear of "contaminating the data," for it was already clear that my task would be to document the contamination rather than to neutralize it. But I knew I should maintain a low profile with the children. I wanted them to view me as a quiet observer rather than as part of the teaching force. And anyhow, I was finding, to my surprise, that observing the children took all my time and energy. What was I to do?

The dilemma of the classroom was often on my mind. For the lack of a solution, I began secretly to watch Mrs. Howard. She wouldn't have wanted me to observe her—I could tell by the way she lowered her voice when I was near. And so I usually sat beside a child, with my ears alert to Mrs. Howard's voice.

I don't think she knew quite what to say to the children about their writing. Sometimes she'd lavishly compliment a child, other times she'd hunt out every error. But usually she avoided interactions and concentrated on the class as a whole. She'd pass out assignments, give children half-sheets of paper (to save trees) and remind them to write with pencils, not mouths. Mostly her attention was on the two ends of composing—assigning topics and correcting mistakes. To me, it was an alien way to teach composition.

As I sat among the children, my chair drawn closely alongside a youngster's desk, I sometimes found myself observing Mrs. Howard more closely than I observed the children. It was a new experience for me to sit in a child's place and to have another woman standing in my place. Then one morning, I began to notice Mrs. Howard noticing me.

An image flashed into mind of the time my sixth graders pressured me to "teach" them dance. They begged and pleaded. Because I was a new teacher, saying no would have been as hard as saying yes. I remember how exposed I felt during those dance classes—exposed on all sides. I felt all hands and feet dancing, and foolish. Being seen by the children was hard enough, and so I kept watching the door, hoping no one would come in and see the chaos and worse, see me. Because I didn't know what else to do, and because I felt out of control, I yelled out commands like an army sergeant.

That moment of empathy became a seed for change. It occurred to me that I would never have allowed a researcher to document my floundering attempts to teach dance. Yet Mrs. Howard had done the equivalent. What courage it must have taken her to invite me, a university researcher, to observe her in the curriculum area of her greatest uncertainty.

I realized she must wonder what I was seeing. Worse, she must sense it: a shake of the head, an early exit from her classroom, silence. What messages had I been sending?

I didn't *decide* to change my stance, for none of this was quite conscious. Somehow, I just began to look through different eyes. I began not only to accept but to cherish that Mrs. Howard was as human as the rest of us. And I began to focus on what children could do, on who they were as individuals, rather than on whether the class met my expectations.

Faces emerged from the crowd. Diane's gentle looks—her long dark hair, greyish green eyes and knack for looking ever so girlish in sweatshirt and jeans. Sometimes Diane brought little presents for Susie, sealing their friendship with a box of raisins, a shared pencil sharpener or a brand-new eraser.

Amy watched on. Usually she was near Susie and Diane, and usually she seemed entirely comfortable with being close enough to participate but distant enough to observe. Dark-eyed Amy was the class artist, and I sometimes wondered if this talent had grounded her in another world. Occasionally she wrote about her big sister or her mother's boyfriend, but mostly she wrote about her creatures: Sidney, her cat; the foxes she drew; the farm she would own someday. From the first, Amy made word pictures with her writing. In fourth grade, she was to begin her fox report like this:

> A beam of light shown through the crack in the fox's den. The red fox opened his eyes just a slit and looked around his den . . .

Craig was the youngster teachers sighed over. "What to do about Craig?" they'd ask each other. Craig wasn't the only child who lacked basic skills in reading and writing, but because of his behavior, he was the most noticeable. It seemed that every day before recess, Craig was warned, and every day after recess, he was scolded. The funny thing about tough guy Craig was that no one hovered near me as much as he did. And when Craig wasn't writing about wars and bloody accidents, he wrote about Blackie, his baby rabbit.

Birger would have been our All-American boy except for the fact that he was Norwegian. He wore rugby shirts and corduroy jeans and he could sit alongside a girl without blushing. That fall, Birger was one of three youngsters to participate in the townwide running race, and he was the only one who wasn't too proud to wave to his mother and his friends.

And Susie. I do not know what it was that drew me to our bright-eyed, soft-spoken heroine. My husband suggests she may have reminded me of myself as a child: the straight dark hair framing her face, the energy that sparkled in her eyes and made others draw close to her. Her friends wore ribbons in their hair and brightly colored parkas, but Susie's tastes were simpler. Her coat was navy blue and she didn't wear any ribbons, yet she sparkled with vitality. Children clustering around her desk told me, "Susie's the one who thinks up good adventures." As I began to know her, I saw it was true.

One morning during recess Susie and Diane peeked their heads into the faculty room. Mrs. Howard beckoned them over. "Can we take paper and pencils outside?" they asked. Diane explained, "Me and Susie found this dead chipmunk and we buried him." Her eyes met Susie's and the two girls nodded with great seriousness. "We want to write a funeral service for him."

Three days later Susie and her cluster of friends asked to stay in during recess. Their plan was first to clean their desks, then to dust the bookcases and reorganize the math tables. Even cleaning became an adventure when Susie was around!

Funny things happened when I began to view the children as individuals rather than thinking only of whether the class met my expectations. Take Susie's clockmaker story. It could be an example of voiceless, conventional writing, but when I looked at it more closely and with trust, I saw it differently. For example, it seemed significant that when the year began, Susie was writing about a man, his wife, cat and dog. Alongside of Susie, Wendy retold a thrilling movie, Craig filled his page with car crashes, Diane sat before an empty page saying, "I can't think of anything exciting enough." But Susie happily spun her tale about a little man who made clocks, worked in his garden, and felt content.

I wondered, too, if it could be significant that Susie's first story was about a clockmaker. As it turned out, the clockmaker's subject—the passage of time—proved also to be Susie's subject. In this story and in later stories, Susie wove her characters into a linear sequence of time. Whereas other children structured their pieces around the visual, Susie's structure tended to be temporal. Thus in her story we read about the sequence of the clockmaker's day but we do not see his shop or the setting of his home. For both Susie and the clockmaker, time becomes the subject of their craft; while the clockmaker measured time with hammer and tin, Susie measured hers with narrative and print.

It was not only Susie but also the "third-grade plateau" which I began to see with new eyes. I'd been quick to name Mrs. Howard the culprit, yet third-grade conventionality extends beyond any one classroom. On the playground, eight- to ten-year-old children are known for their rigid adherence to rules. It is the age of "the right way to play." In their oral language, children of this age group stay close to the literal meaning of words. (A third-grade teacher recently asked her children to clap the dirty chalkboard erasers against each other. The youngsters went outside and returned to the classroom a few minutes later, covered with rectangular prints of chalk dust.) In their art work, stock characters and themes replace an earlier exploratory flavor. Howard Gardner summarizes the middle childhood years by saying, "Now, for the first time, a child in the midst of singing or dancing will stop and nervously ask, 'Is this right?'" (1980, p. 150).

And so, by late September, I'd realized that it was too easy to put all the blame on Mrs. Howard. I began to suspect that Susie's attention to convention and correctness probably related to development as well as to environment. By the third grade, children have a growing ability to anticipate a future time, to envision their work existing in a different context. When they write, they can plan ahead and they can anticipate a distant audience's response. They can also look back at their texts and view them through someone else's eyes.

Growing up means acquiring new powers, but it also means learning new fears. As young children develop their ability to review and judge their writing, they can become more deliberate, but also more self-conscious. As they develop their ability to see their work through the eyes of another, they can become more conscious of the needs of their audience, but also more aware of peer pressure, more afraid of being different. As they develop more ability to plan, they also become more able to worry.

Middle childhood is a vulnerable time for most children. Susie and her classmates seemed to have retreated to the safety of conventional, correct pieces. Yet I was sensing this could be a time of potential as well as of risk. The same forces which make this a vulnerable time, could also make it a powerful time. I was looking forward to watching Susie's growth, confident something would happen.

3. A partnership forms

My research didn't feel like spying anymore, and I wasn't so afraid of looking Mrs. Howard in the eye. Rather than detouring around her, I began coming to school early to tag along as she ran off dittos and prepared the classroom. We talked about her exercise class and my struggles to write, but mostly we talked about the children. It was such a luxury to have someone else who was interested in their every move. In the staff room, we'd pull our chairs together and puzzle over their stories, delighting in them and looking altogether like an elderly couple with pictures of the grandchildren.

Sometimes as we leafed through the children's writing, Pat would ask, "Did you see Birger write this piece?" or "What were Amy and Rebecca talking about today?" Sometimes I'd ask her questions, and from time to time, I'd make suggestions. At first the other teachers in the staff room would eye us from across the table. They'd listen for a moment, then shake their heads and resume their conversations.

In the classroom, Pat and I began to help each other observe and enjoy the children. When Birger brought his paper to her, instead of red inking each of his exclamation marks, she and the youngster counted them. "I was trying to add excitement," Birger explained, and so they called me over and we reread the story looking for alternative ways to add excitement. (See *Fig. 3.1*)

Pat Howard and I worried about Aaron together, for he'd gone days without putting a single word onto his paper. Often as we worked across the room from each other, our eyes would meet and we'd both look over at Aaron who sat, his face in his hands. In the middle of one writing session, Pat motioned for me to look at Aaron's paper. On the top of the page, in painful cramped letters, the boy had written:

I doent lik to rit

That day, Aaron's friends met in writing groups to share their work with each other. Energy for writing was high. At the end of the session, I saw that Aaron had added a single word to his paper. Pat and I celebrated what he had written:

I doent lik to rit Today

Fig. 3.1

When I can't BReth!

I could't talk! I was tring to

say, "I cant breth!"
I fell on a rock! my side hert!
I got up, I started jumping

up and down! I fill like I m
my stamock fllt nome, going blow a hostatted
I was scared! I started brething

again!

We watched Susie too, and marveled at the magnetic pull the pixielike girl held over her more sophisticated friends. After school, Pat told me what she knew of the Sible family. "You see all four of them together a lot," she said. "When I drive by their house, the parents are often on the lawn with Susie and Jill. They are the sort of family that even go to the grocery store together."

We were learning to read children's writing in a new way, seeing the printed words as the tip of an iceberg and speculating what might lie under the surface. Sometimes I'd dismiss a piece of writing and then Mrs. Howard would see things in it; sometimes it was the other way around. For both of us, it was new to intently puzzle over each piece of writing, looking for what it revealed about the writer. Sometimes there seemed to be no pattern at all to children's errors. We looked for a long time, for example, at Craig's first piece of writing before we could learn from it. (See *Fig. 3.2*, p. 22)

Only when we trusted that Craig's mistakes as well as his successes were indications of what he knew did we find clues to the thinking between the lines. We wondered if the rise and fall of Craig's printing reflected the lilt of his oral language. Were capitals used for emphasis? How had he dared to attempt such words as emergency (amercks)? When questions such as these guided our observations, instead of being the cause of despair, Craig became the cause of concern and soon, of hope.

Fig. 3.2

I was Divnin the seRwoLand as an
to caRS cRashngan Ianstcroshing rot into.
trcmB utI tuRnedoua gandthanI TuRned
Satowt To get away andathy then 5 moRegaRS
cRas heing 9bt beh + neam ect scaRcmsg

Translation

I was driving the steering wheel and all of a sudden two cars
crashed. I almost crashed right into them but I turned away and
then I turned straight to get away and then five more cars crashed
and then the emergency car came . . .

We rarely talked directly about curriculum or about the teaching of writing. I shied away from those topics, not because I had
no suggestions to make, but because I knew that as a live-in guest
in room 209, I needed to be Mrs. Howard's friend and colleague
rather than her supervisor. Occasionally I did make suggestions
"for research purposes" knowing full well my intent was to
influence her teaching. But mostly, it was enough to talk about
the children and about their learning, for our intense focus on the
children was leading implicitly to changes in the classroom environment and in Mrs. Howard's approaches toward teaching writing. Neither Mrs. Howard nor I consciously directed those changes;
we certainly had no thought, at the time, that room 209 would
become a model writing classroom, and that our joint efforts
would lead not only to data on how children learn to write, but
also to data on how teachers can facilitate that learning.

Since the study, many people have questioned my role in Mrs.
Howard's classroom. "Do you mean Mrs. Howard changed magically without guidance from you?" I do not know how to answer
their questions. Clearly it was not by accident that the classroom
became more like the British primary schools in which I'd done
my training. Yet the approach toward teaching writing which
was developed in that classroom, and also in Mrs. Currier's
fourth grade, was not my invention, nor did it belong to Don
Graves or Susan Sowers whose attention focused on first and
second grade classrooms. And yes, it did seem magical. Changes
in the curriculum, like the movement on a Ouiji board, seemed to
arise magically out of a shared focus on how children learn to
write.

If only there'd been another set of researchers at Atkinson documenting the interactions between our research team and the teachers, for clearly each party had left a powerful impact on the other. If only there'd been another researcher in room 209, documenting the changes in both Mrs. Howard and me. Since my attention was soon so focused on the children, Mrs. Howard's growth became the backdrop, affecting my data as lighting affects the painter's subject. In retrospect, I often replay those first few months in the classroom, asking myself, "How did the changes in the classroom and in Mrs. Howard happen?" and "Which were the turnkey changes that led to others?"

I think that, especially because I was in room 209 not as a co-teacher but as a researcher, my presence highlighted the importance of Mrs. Howard's role. My respectful interest in every little thing her children did validated the importance of her profession. Mrs. Howard and only Mrs. Howard could create the environment in which children would grow as writers. This is the awesome responsibility every teacher knows, a responsibility which often goes unrecognized by the outside world and eventually by the teachers themselves. By highlighting the importance of Mrs. Howard's teaching, the research project helped her regain the sense of personal mission which had led her into the teaching profession nine years before. It had eroded over the years, but now the NIE study had rekindled in her the belief that she had a unique contribution she could make to her students.

When our study was completed, Dr. Bob Walshe of Australia asked Graves, "What is the essential message of your study?" Graves replied, "When people own a place, they look after it. When it belongs to someone else, they couldn't care less." Graves was referring to children and their ownership of a piece of writing, but his words apply also to teachers and their ownership of their teaching. When Mrs. Howard began to feel responsibility and ownership for her classroom, she began to look after it, to invest herself in it. During school time and after school, she began to think of ways she could help children grow as writers. Looking back, I can see that she made three essential changes in her writing program during the first few months. These changes will be the subject of the next few chapters, for unless we look at changes in the classroom context it will be hard to understand the changes in Susie's writing.

4. Topics which tap the energy to write

During the first few weeks of school, I watched Susie come into the classroom each morning full of stories about washing her dog, shopping with her mother, feeding worms to a bird. She'd tell the stories to Diane before attendance was taken, and often she'd finish them on hidden bits of paper, passed secretly from writer to reader. But when writing time came, with assignments to write about summer vacations and magic machines, Susie's urge to share information was gone. I began to wonder about assigned topics. Did they distract children from the concerns of the moment? Did they steer children from writing with voice and information?

The questions reminded me of an almost humorous incident. A year or two earlier, I'd watched children clamber off a school bus at the zoo. The youngsters skipped and danced, wide-eyed at the sight of giraffes and elephants. Then their teacher called out, "Children, don't forget, we're looking at feet!"

I never made my youngsters write about feet, but had my well-intentioned topics—"An Embarrassing Moment," "My Favorite Trip"—been equally distracting? One time I'd knocked a hornet's nest off the garage roof and proudly brought it to school, suggesting the children write about my trophy. Was I assuming they didn't have their own trophies to write about? I used to wonder why my topics didn't work. Now, as I watched Susie and the others, I wondered if the problem had been that my topics were just that—mine.

I fretted over whether to mention my concern to Pat Howard. The culminating incident occurred when she asked her children to write on lost dolphins—a topic listed in their Language Arts textbook. Because her children knew little, if anything, about dolphins, their stories tended to read, "Once upon a time there was a lost dolphin. He was lonely," and then they'd proceed to tell how the dolphin found its mother or father or whomever. When Mrs. Howard and I leafed through those twenty-six stories, I was tempted to say something like "Circle the one that's different."

Mrs. Howard saved the day. "That was a stupid assignment," she said. "I wonder if it would work better if they choose their own topics?" I wanted to hug her.

I couldn't wait for the next writing workshop, for the chance to see Susie and the others put into writing the news they shared so eagerly each morning. But when Mrs. Howard told the children, "Today you can write about anything you want," the room grew strangely silent.

"Anything? But—like what?" one child asked anxiously.

"Whatever you know and care about," Mrs. Howard answered. "The things that are important to you."

The children remained unconvinced and uncomfortable. Graves describes a similar moment by saying, "Children who are fed topics, story starters, lead sentences . . . as a steady diet . . . rightfully panic when topics have to come from them. The anxiety is not unlike that of the child whose mother has just turned off the television set. 'Now what do I do?' bellows the child. Suddenly their acts depend on them and they are unused to providing their own motivations and direction" (1982, p. 21).

Several of Mrs. Howard's children dealt with the void by recalling story starters from previous years. Others managed to invent "exciting enough" ideas. (It seemed that the children had watched so much television they were convinced a story had to contain a murder, suicide and crime or it wasn't "exciting enough.") But after a few days of these self-selected topics, the children began to run dry. One boy told me, "You run out of exciting things to write about." Then he added, "I mean, I already wrote about a car crash, a murder and this wicked bad fight. What else is there?"

When Mrs. Howard and I watched children sit face-to-face with the empty page, we realized what we, as a profession, had done. When teachers dole out topics, children become dependent on them. And so now Mrs. Howard's students weren't so sure they wanted to be taken off writer's welfare, for they'd come to believe they had no writing territory, no turf of their own. They'd come to believe their lives and their ideas weren't worth writing about.

Mrs. Howard and I talked about the problem in the lunchroom. This time, other teachers participated in our conversations. By the time I left school at 3:45 that day, a cluster of teachers had gathered outside the front office to talk about ways to help children realize their ideas, concerns and information were worth putting into print.

When Susie and her classmates arrived at school the next morning, they found their desks pushed against the back wall and a ring of chairs facing the chalkboard. Alongside the chalkboard Mrs. Howard had hung three X-ray pictures. Two pieces of chalk and twenty-six children waited.

"Today, class," Mrs. Howard said, "I have . . . um . . . I have a story." She took a deep breath and stepped up to the chalkboard. She looked nervous standing there, and strangely out of place where she usually fit so naturally. "Last night I thought about your writing," she said, "and I figured I might try writing too. I thought about telling about my last haircut, or the new fern that's growing outside my door," she said, carefully using little everyday topics for her examples, "but I finally decided on my topic," and turning to the large X-rays which hung beside her, she added, "If you interview me about my X-rays, you can help me know what I have to say."

"Is that you in those X-rays?" Amy wanted to know.

"No, it's my dog," the teacher answered, disappointing several boys who'd been trying to spot the breasts on the greyish black film. Now the dark shadows on the X-rays raised new questions.

"What happened to your dog?" The children inched their chairs closer and listened, captivated by their teacher's story and, more importantly, by the fact that she was sharing it with them. The children missed snack time that day but no one seemed to mind. Mrs. Howard had tapped their energy—and her own.

The following day a large plastic robot greeted me at the door to room 209. "He's mine," eight-year-old Michael said. "Mrs. Howard told us it was our turn to bring something special from home and now me and Craig are interviewing about my robot."

"Ms. Calkins." I turned and found that the small voice was calling me from inside a large Polynesian mask. The masked figure darted off into the roomful of treasures, each more elaborate than the next.

On the fringes of the classroom, Diane and Susie whispered together, oblivious to the rest of the room. For her treasure, Susie had brought a scrappy little bird's nest. As she carefully pulled it from her parka pocket, Susie told Diane about finding the nest. Other children heard their giggles and they, too, clustered around the simple little nest, each with his or her own story to tell of finding a bird's nest, of watching eggs hatch. Across the room, a giant plastic robot and a Polynesian mask lay on two empty desks.

I didn't realize it at the time, but this little incident foreshadowed Susie's role in her third- and fourth-grade classrooms. Over the next two years, her unpretentious, easy enthusiasm would wield a powerful influence on her classmates. In her unselfconscious way, Susie led other youngsters to take pleasure also in life's small treasures. It was not unusual for one or another of Susie's classmates to tell me, "I have more to write about when I play with Susie because we do such fun things." Then when I questioned more closely, the great adventures turned out to be small everyday things—shampooing the dog, or throwing birdseed in each other's hair and pretending they were brides.

After Susie, Diane and the others who'd joined them finished their interview over the bird's nest, and the youngsters headed back to their desks to begin writing about their treasures, Susie said to me, "I know my bird's nest isn't too big a thing, but sometimes I think the little things that are close to you are the most important of all." Over the next two years, Susie would often use writing to frame the little things in her life, bringing meaning and significance to them. She would write about getting a teddy bear for her birthday, snuggling with her father, and sailing worms on walnut-shell boats. Once Susie said to me, "I think the reason I can write is because all these special things happen to me and I keep seeing stories in them." She continued, "Like last night, I was in my pajamas and then my father said, 'The stars are out,' and asked if I wanted to go for a ride with him on the moped . . . and when I was riding along, pretending I was blind, so many stories kept coming to me." The girl looked at me and with great seriousness said, "I wonder if everyone has such a special life as I do."

The day Susie and her classmates brought their treasures into school and interviewed each other to learn their stories was perhaps the single most important turning point in the study. As we move on through the next two years, it will be evident that never again would Mrs. Howard try to motivate children by assigning them to write on her topics. Instead, her role changed. She started seeing her task as helping the children know their lives and ideas were worth writing about. She became a listener.

Often she'd meet the children before school as they tumbled off the school bus. Perhaps Diane had a map of her summer trip; Geoff, an invitation to Eric's birthday party; and Craig, plans for Blackie's new rabbit hutch. When children learned these could be topics for writing, their topic choice was rarely a problem.

Then, too, Mrs. Howard and I took notice of the treasures carried in lunch bags and parka pockets. We cleared a shelf and made a display case. The "clean tooth" display was replaced with photographs from Diane's trip. Graves once said to me, "You can tell a good writing classroom by the presence of the child's interests in the room." Room 209 was on its way to becoming a good writing classroom.

Although Pat Howard didn't know it, at the University of New Hampshire my writing teacher was also insisting that students select their own topics and write from their lives. Donald M. Murray, a Pulitzer Prize-winning writer and the guiding light in our study, describes one day of his teaching this way:

> It was dark when I arrived at my office this winter morning, and it is dark again as I wait for my last writing student to step out of the shadows in the corridor for my last conference. I am tired but it is a good tired, for my students have generated energy as well as absorbed it. I've learned something of what it is to be a childhood diabetic, to raise oxen, to be a welfare mother with three children, to build a bluebird trail, . . . to bring your father home to die of cancer. I have been instructed in other lives, heard the voices of my students they had not heard before, shared their satisfaction in solving the problems of writing with clarity and grace. . . .I hear voices from my students they have never heard from themselves. I find they are authorities on subjects they think are ordinary. . . .It is a matter of faith. Faith that my students have something to say and a language in which to say it. (1979, pp. 13, 15)

I had expected that when children chose their own topics, they would become more invested in writing. But I hadn't expected the changes which became apparent in their written products. Now that the children were writing about everyday events in their lives, they used telling details, and wrote with specific concrete information. Instead of writing about a lost dolphin or an unknown man who got up at 8:00 and had breakfast at 8:30, Susie would soon write about learning to play baseball and about seeing a deer alongside the road. In Chapter 9, the difference these new topics made in her writing will be evident.

Not all children found it easy to select good topics, and most children learned through trial and error. Gina tried to write about her grandmother's trip to Chinatown and eventually abandoned the topic, saying, "Grandma could write about it but I can't." Brad tried to write about an anticipated football game, but soon decided the topic would work better after the game took place. The biggest problem children faced was that they often chose giant, sweeping areas of interest rather than focused topics. When Mrs. Howard gathered the class together and asked what each planned to write about, invariably a youngster would say "my life." Other favorite topics were equally broad: my cousin, my trip, school, summer.

"Of all that you have to say about your summer, what's the one most important thing you want to focus on?" Mrs. Howard would ask, and eventually children learned to whittle their topics down to size.

Then, too, most children went through dry periods. "Nothing happens to me," they'd moan. "I'm broke. I'm clear out of topics." For some children, it helped to keep a running list of possible topics on the inside cover of their writing folders. For others, it was enough to brainstorm ideas on scrap paper, to talk with a friend, to free write, or to listen in on their friends' topics until a good one came to mind. In any case, topic choice was in the hands of the writer. For a time, children were encouraged to write what they knew and cared about, and so personal narratives and informal reports were the dominant mode of writing. Fiction, letters, content-area reports, and poetry would come later.

5. The structure of a writing workshop

When the year began, writing was squeezed into fifteen-minute time slots. The entire school day was like that: a collage of little bits. Ten minutes for spelling, fifteen minutes for a quiz. Ten minutes for a penmanship ditto. Twenty minutes for page 36 in the social studies text. Graves likened the schedule to driving in city traffic: the children shifted from first to second gear, but never got into high gear for there were no broad stretches of time.

The children's writing reflected the staccato rhythm of the classroom. Youngsters whipped off papers in quick bursts, writing without much forethought or deliberation. "Get it done" seemed to be the motto. The pace is one we all know well, for ours is a first-draft-only society, a land of frozen waffles, easy divorces, of commercials every seven minutes. Detachment is built into a time-frame such as this. No wonder the children wrote in September on topics in which they had no investment. There was no time for investment, for sustainment. There was no time for doing one's best, then making one's best better.

Writing well, as we were to learn, requires a different pace than we are used to in our schools. The initial fifteen-minute writing slot was stretched into twenty minutes, then thirty, forty. By the middle of October, Mrs. Howard's children spent three or four hours a week in writing workshop and then, to get even more time, they sometimes elected to write during recess.

The chipmunk's funeral had been the first time Susie and Diane asked to bring pencils and paper onto the playground during recess. Soon they didn't bother to ask. Diane and Susie wrote the script for a puppet show during three consecutive recesses, and then spent hours of time at home making the puppets. When Susie wrote a story for her sister's birthday present, that, too, was written during recess. "You need to have all the time you want for a piece of writing," Susie once told a visitor to her classroom. "Otherwise you're afraid to look back, afraid to see that it's not what you wanted, that it's not all you could do."

Time was all the more valuable if it was regular, scheduled time, for then the children could plan for writing. They could think about their writing at home, as Amy did in devising the lead to her fox report. "I was lying in my bed, just thinking and thinking. I heard my sister come home. She went into her room and closed the door," she said, adding, "A beam of light shone through the crack in her door, and when my cat Sidney looked up, it made her squint." Amy continued, "So I thought of how to start my report and I held it in my head 'till I got to school."

Debbie also rehearsed for writing when she was at home. "Sometimes if I'm stuck on what to write about, if I know writing will be the next day, I get my Mom to help me. When I was a little girl I used to sing all these songs and here I am, in chorus. So my Mom last night starts singing the songs and it refreshes my memory and I'm ready for writing time."

As the schedule for Mrs. Howard's classroom became predictable, the children began writing as if there was a tomorrow. "I'll just write it fast," Susie would say, "and tomorrow I'll read it over." By late October, Mrs. Howard's children were writing every Monday, Wednesday and Friday from 9:10 to 10:30. Soon, not only the schedule for writing but also the agenda within each writing workshop, was predictable. Writing always began with a ten-minute mini-lesson, followed by a fifty-minute workshop for writing and conferences, followed by some method of sharing work-in-process. When other teachers heard about this consistent routine, they were surprised. "Isn't it boring to do the same thing each day?" "Don't you need to change things, to motivate the kids?"

I sympathized with their questions and so did Pat. We'd each entered the school year believing creative writing required a creative classroom structure; earlier in the year and in preceding years, Pat's writing sessions had been a kaleidoscope of new approaches and agendas.

Things had begun to change when Pat wanted time to observe and work with individual youngsters. "I don't want to spend my time choreographing," she said. She'd already built consistent structures into reading time so she could work with individuals— now she did the same during writing.

Eventually we realized this structure was not only helpful to Pat, it was also helpful to the children. "Creative" classroom structures do not give children freedom, as we might suppose, any more than do "creative bedtime hours." When classroom environments are always changing, always haphazard, this not only puts teachers into the position of choreographing, it also puts children into the position of waiting for their teachers' changing agendas.

Mrs. Howard found that it was important not only to have a predictable timetable for writing, but also to have consistent expectations—or, more bluntly, rules. Marion Howe, a writing process teacher from New York who has learned from Mrs. Howard's work, recently explained the ironic importance of having a few, simple rules.

> Because I insist all children are involved in the writing process during writing time, I can give children the freedom to move naturally and independently between rehearsal, drafting, revision and editing. Because I insist that when one piece is finished, another is begun, I do not have to set class deadlines. Because children know all final work must be edited, they can edit when they are ready. Because I insist children do not disturb others with their peer conferences and because I've taught them how to have productive conferences, the kids can talk together with whomever, whenever they need help.

It is significant to realize the most creative environments in our society are not the ever-changing ones. The artist's studio, the researcher's laboratory, and the scholar's library are each deliberately kept simple so as to support the complexities of the work-in-progress. They are deliberately kept predictable, so the unpredictable can happen. Similarly, Mrs. Howard and I became convinced that the juxtaposition of a complex, changing craft such as writing and a simple consistent environment freed the children to make choices as they wrote.

6. Editing: last but not least

Although it had been Pat Howard's idea to let children choose their own topics, it was my idea to postpone corrections until the end of the writing process. I wasn't willing to wait for Pat to discover for herself that editing could be postponed until after drafting and revision. And so one morning in late September, as Mrs. Howard and I sat in her classroom with her ever-present plastic container of coffee on the table in front of us, I gathered my courage and began. I approached the subject with delicacy, suggesting that perhaps Pat might try emphasizing spelling and punctuation a little less in the first drafts . . .

"I know, I know," she said, laughing as she interrupted my carefully planned presentation. She didn't need my reasons since she'd recently watched her own daughter Amy write "big" when she wanted to say "enormous." And she'd seen the word-by-word writing in her classroom. As we talked about it, she agreed that word-by-word writing probably destroys fluency just as word-by-word reading destroys comprehension. And so in Susie's third-grade classroom—and later, in classrooms throughout Atkinson Elementary School—children were told not to worry over their spelling and punctuation until their pieces were done.

Telling the children this was one thing, following through on it was another. Pat was willing—but it wasn't easy for her. "My hands are sore from sitting on them," she joked with me. "But it's the only way I can keep from wielding my red pen." It wasn't easy for her to read children's writing listening to the message rather than looking for the errors. "My one purpose in reading their papers used to be to find their mistakes," she explained.

The children didn't know whether to trust Mrs. Howard when she told them correctness didn't matter in early drafts. It helped a little when we showed them my messy, incomplete drafts. But I think it helped the children even more when we gave editing its place in the writing process. Mrs. Howard set up an editing table in the back of the classroom and children learned that when their pieces were finished, they could go to the editing table and, using checklists and red pens, underline spelling errors, check for missing words, correct punctuation and so forth. Some checklists directed attention to other problem areas as well: paragraphing, precise word choice, clarity.

The editing checklists and procedures changed somewhat over the course of the study. New items were added to the list and old ones removed. A special list was developed for Craig who often felt overwhelmed by the chaos of errors on his paper. Another list was developed for children who excelled in the mechanics of writing: Alan, Trish and Wendy. For a few months, Mrs. Howard asked children to collaborate with a peer editor, but when this encouraged children to criticize each other, the plan was abandoned. Instead children were to bring their edited pieces to their teacher for her corrections before they copied them onto white paper. But this led to new problems: a huge backlog of children formed. Eventually Mrs. Howard put a box labled *For Final Editing* on the editing table. During the rest of the year, youngsters stapled their checklists onto their corrected drafts and left them in the crate. Then they could move on to their next piece of writing while waiting for a final editing conference.

As soon as she had time, Mrs. Howard met with the children individually to go over their writing. No matter how many errors still glared at her, she tried to begin editing conferences by supporting what children *had* done. In time the children learned that they could count on these conferences to be largely positive, that they needn't approach them in fear and trembling. Mrs. Howard especially tried to appreciate the new things children tried, whether rightly or wrongly; the risks they had taken. "I want them to be willing to try new things," she said. Once, as I watched her reading a story, she came to a line which said:

I got a model from:Eric.

"Oh! You've used a colon the first time!" was her first response, followed by the question, "How'd you go about deciding to use it in this particular place?"

I drew closer, eager to hear the writer's rationale. Mrs. Howard and I had learned together that there were good reasons for most errors. "You know, like on a birthday card," Brad answered. "To: Brad, From: Eric."

We appreciated Brad's way of thinking, and then Mrs. Howard gave him a quick lesson on the colon. That was the rhythm of every editing conference. A few minutes to appreciate what the writer *had* done, a few minutes to teach something new. One day she might teach paragraphing, another day, quotation marks. Whenever Mrs. Howard figured she'd gotten enough mileage out of a child's draft, she'd simply correct the remaining errors (with blue pen or pencil) and the writer was ready for a final draft.

"At first I worried this was an inefficient way to teach mechanics," Mrs. Howard says in retrospect. "But if you think about it, the *really* inefficient way is what we'd been doing all along—teaching quotation marks in third grade, fourth grade, fifth, sixth, seventh grade . . . with children never learning them."

When editing skills are taught in the context of a child's own writing, they are learned as well as taught. Children pass the information along to each other. Mrs. Howard explained ellipses to one youngster and soon these enigmatic dots were being used throughout the classroom. "These dots; they mean one, two, three minutes went by," one girl told me. She'd begun her paper like this:

RRR . . . the alarm clock woke me up.

By February of that year, the children were using punctuation marks so easily and well, I decided to collect more extensive data on this editing skill. I interviewed Pat Howard's third graders and also, for contrast, the third graders from Mrs. West's room across the hall. Mrs. West described her program this way. "I start at the beginning, teaching them simple sentences, periods, and capitals. Everything that is in the book. I do a whole lesson on it." She often wrote sentences on the chalkboard and asked her children to insert the missing punctuation. She made dittos on question marks, and gave tests before and after each lesson. Her children rarely wrote and when they did, Mrs. West vigilantly red penned each error. "If I find a bit of missing punctuation, it is five points off," she said. "After a couple 50s, with big red periods all down the page, they learn." In Pat Howard's classroom, the children learned editing skills through writing, and they relegated the concern for correctness to the end of the writing process.

In my punctuation mark study, I asked each child from the two classrooms to tell me what each mark meant and how it was used. I found that Pat's third graders could explain an average of more than eight kinds of punctuation. The children from Mrs. West's room, who had studied punctuation through classwork, drills and tests, but had rarely written, were able to explain fewer than four kinds.

"I like punctuation," Birger explained. "It lets you know where the sentence ends, so otherwise one minute you'd be sledding down the hill and the next minute you'd be inside the house, without even stopping."

Fewer than twenty-five percent of the children in the mechanics classroom—Mrs. West's room—liked punctuation. "Punctuation is embarrassing," one nine-year-old told me. "You forget what it is for."

When children write, they don't forget what punctuation is

for. This is Wendy's statement on commas: "If you have a long sentence and you want to keep it all there, you put a comma in to take a breath. If you were to make a new sentence, you'd change it up. One example is my last piece of writing. I said, 'We got a little lower and over the beach, I saw tiny colored dots.' Before and after the comma, they are parts of the same sentence. Like the first half of the sentence is one paragraph, and the other half is the second paragraph . . . like two edges of the same idea."

The effectiveness of this approach to editing was nowhere more evident than in the changes in the writing of the less able students in Mrs. Howard's classroom. This is Craig's writing, less than three months after his story about the two cars crashing:

Goofy the cowboy   Dec 18

When goofy was a little boy,
every body teosed him. An he
grew up being teosed. Goofy had
funny ears and funny nose and
Legs. And he didn't Like it a
bit. Then he started to get
mad Then!! he got some guns
and had fun. And killed a few
People. But he didn't care a bit.
He was Having fun. Then he
was the king of the Village. And
had a blast. No body would teosed
him any more. Then the people
of the village made a law, you
couldn't kill any body. And goofy
got mad and disobey and Went
to Jail.

7. The teacher's role

Butterflies grow through metamorphosis, but for human beings, change is usually not so sudden. Instead, it happens in bits and pieces, in spurts and plateaus. Pat Howard had not changed overnight. She still gave spelling tests every Friday; she still taught social studies through dittos and textbooks. Her children still read Basal readers rather than library books. Although desks were arranged in clusters rather than rows and children's projects lined the edges of the classroom, many things had not changed. The day was still compartmentalized into separate subjects; the curriculum still followed textbooks; and the children still worked silently much of the time. Writing was the exception, not the new rule. Mrs. Howard's teaching had become a combination of contrasts—of teacher-directed and child-centered, of skills-in-context and skills-in-isolation.

These polarities never went away, not that year, anyhow. The visitors who came to see Mrs. Howard's classroom often commented afterward to me that it was strange to see children learning through interaction, through pacing their own work, through using skills in the context of writing . . . and yet to see this against the backdrop of a chalkboard full of references to workbooks, Basal readers, dittos.

I used to wish the polarities would ease away, that child-centered learning would replace teacher-directed instruction. But Pat had a firm grounding in traditional approaches to teaching—and I was not around to support changes during her social studies, science, and reading classes.

Although I would have preferred it had Pat made a radical and complete transformation, visitors to the classroom were heartened to see that a traditional teacher, well-steeped in textbooks, workbooks and prepackaged curricula, could lead such a successful writing workshop. In fact, the assistant superintendent from the Guilderland, New York, school system recently recalled her visit to Atkinson, saying, "What impressed me the most was not Mrs. Giacobbe's wonderful first grade—we all know there are remarkable teachers who can do remarkable things." Then she added, "What impressed me most were the other classrooms, where I saw very traditional teachers doing very remarkable things."

In truth, Pat Howard's grounding in teacher-directed instruction was probably part of the success of her writing workshop. Because she was accustomed to being an integral part of her student's learning, she was never tempted simply to set children free. This was important, for by late October the children didn't need their teacher in the way they had earlier. They chose their own topics, regulated their own pace, and were audiences for each other. They didn't need Mrs. Howard to prod and cajole them into writing or to silence them with the approaching click of her heels. How easy it would have been for Mrs. Howard to bask in her success, and then to correct math papers during the writing workshop! But she had never been an advocate of the "set children free" philosophy. And so—quite unconsciously—she set out to find a new place for herself in the writing workshop.

Two factors seemed to shape the new identity which emerged. One was Pat Howard's participation in the research. I suspect that the content of what she learned from the youngsters was less important than that she was learning from them. She approached children wanting to understand their thinking. "What problems are you trying to solve?" she'd ask. "How did you go about doing this?" "What questions are puzzling you?"

These are unusual things for teachers to ask. We are more apt to seek solutions than problems, and to see our role as delivering answers rather than as posing challenges. Yet the research had given Mrs. Howard a new appreciation for the thinking behind not only their writing, but all the children did. One morning Pat brought in a picture her six-year-old daughter had drawn. "Look at it closely," she urged as she showed it to me. "What do you notice?"

Before I had chance to study the picture, Pat pointed out that underneath the crossed out section, she could see the hint of letters TRKO TRT. "See!" she said with excitement. "The guy is

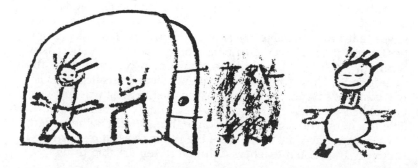

saying trick-or-treat and he's ringing this doorbell" (and she pointed to the dot in the door) "and this is the candy bowl with the pieces of candy." In a similar manner, Pat and I squinted to read the crossed out sections on the children's drafts and speculated about the thinking between their lines. And so it was quite natural that, during writing time, Pat moved around the classroom asking children to tell her about their writing and nudging them on to new challenges.

There was another factor which influenced Pat's teaching that year. Because we worked so closely together, she began to share not only the research project, but also my interest in writing. Sometimes I'd read portions of a rough draft to her, and tell her about my conferences with Don Murray. I told her also about our writing group at the University of New Hampshire. On Tuesday evenings, fifteen of us met together to hear each other's work-in-process and to offer suggestions to each other.

"What kind of suggestions do they make to you?" Pat sometimes asked, and then I'd realize that actually, help usually came in the form of questions. Mostly by asking questions—like "How do you feel about your draft?" "What are you trying to get at?" "What will you do next?" "What discoveries are you making?" and "How can we help?"—people helped me articulate what I wanted to say in an article, how I felt about the draft, and what I planned to do next.

And so, in an indirect way, the writing community at the University of New Hampshire became part of Pat's thinking and teaching. She tried her hand at writing too—little pieces, written to share with her students. From me and from firsthand experience, she developed a feel for the writing process.

Both our research and her own involvement in writing, then, had a part in shaping Mrs. Howard's new role as a writing teacher. She wanted to engage the children in their writing and to give them the time, support and tools to explore and develop their craft. She spent most of the workshop time moving between the desks, working with individuals and with impromptu clusters of children. Watching her, I was reminded of the circus stunt man who sets plates spinning on the ends of long sticks and then steps back to watch. When a plate begins to wobble, the circus man moves over and with his fingertip he gives the plate more spin, then steps back again. "Keep it up," Mrs. Howard would say. "Craig, are you working?" "Renee, why don't you read it to Diane?" "Jeremy, can I help you?" With light touches, she kept her plates spinning. These brief conferences made it possible for longer conferences to also take place.

Conferring seemed so simple at the time, a natural minuet of listening and response, of watching and extending. Mrs. Howard didn't deliberate over what questions to ask anymore than we plan how to respond when we meet a friend. We just ask, "How are you doing?" and then listen and follow where the conversation leads.

Yet now when I work with teachers, I often find learning to hold productive conferences poses more problems than anything else. Teachers want to know how to begin a conference; they ask for a list of questions which will lead to revision; they wonder how long a conference should last. I shake my head and wonder if it really helps to analyze Mrs. Howard's conferences, to take apart what seemed so flowing and easy. When I have time with these teachers, I do not talk about conferences so much as I try to engage them in their own case-study research and writing. For I suspect conferring is only hard for teachers when it does not emerge naturally out of an interest in children's thinking and out of their own involvement in writing.

In time, Pat Howard and I became very conscious of "the art of conferencing." We eventually theorized together about why some conferences are more effective than others, and we even compiled a list of productive questions to ask during conferences. But none of this happened until we were well into the study. The awareness of conferring as a technique emerged only because the visitors who came through the classroom continually asked, "How do you know what questions to ask in a conference?"

Later, we'll look at some of our answers to this question, but for now it is enough to say that at first Pat Howard didn't know what questions to ask. Neither did I. Pat simply felt her way along. She asked questions and made suggestions based on her interest in children's thinking, on her growing trust in their ability to make choices, and on her commitment to helping them experiment during writing.

But first let's go backward in time, and begin to follow the changes in Susie's writing which had occurred during all these changes in the classroom.

II.

One child's growth in writing

8. First lessons

When I arrived in the classroom on September 18th, Diane's and Amy's chairs were pulled close to Susie's desk and they were listening as Susie read them the latest addition to her story.

"How long is it?" Diane asked when Susie stopped reading her story, which bore the proud title "My Lin Su Book." Susie glowed at Diane's interest in the length. Like a true friend, Diane had asked just the right question.

Susie didn't need to count—she'd numbered each page of her writing as if it were a real book. But she counted anyway, starting with her "Table of Contents." "Six!" she announced. Although some of Susie's classmates were more fluent and probably more skillful than she was, none of them had undertaken a project such as the "Lin Su Book." Instead, during the still brief writing sessions, they'd written short pieces—the kind that could be started and finished in a twenty-minute writing workshop. Susie, meanwhile, had persisted on her book for almost a week. With her usual spirit, Susie had created a project for herself.

Neither Mrs. Howard nor I had intervened in the "Lin Su Book," but we had both watched Susie writing it. Each day she would reread the last lines from her previous entry and then add on and on. Her process—and her product—resembled a chain. Writing for her involved moving on, a forward motion.

Of course, there was a reason why I noticed this forward motion more than I noticed other details. The way Susie held her pen, the number and length of her pauses, and the subvocalizations that accompanied her writing were not as interesting to me as the issue of revision. This is because my perspective as a researcher had been influenced by current issues in the field of writing. It seemed that everyone was talking about writing in terms of either prewriting, writing and rewriting, or of rehearsal, drafting, revision and editing. The number and names of the stages differed, but most agreed that writing was more than adding words on and on down the page. And so I was very aware that in September, Susie rarely even reread her text and never revised her content.

The first time Mrs. Howard and Susie had a writing conference was on September 23rd. On that morning, Mrs. Howard asked Susie to reread a page of her "Lin Su" story, circling misspellings. It was a simple intervention, intended only as a lesson in spelling, yet it became one of those happy accidents of teaching. As Susie circled her way down the page she took important steps toward learning that writing involves shuttling between moving forward and stepping back, between being passion-hot and critic-cold.

Consider the implications of those circles. Each circle marred the paper, implying that the work was not finished. Each circle suggested that writing could be a messy craft. More importantly, for the first time, it was Susie's responsibility to mark up her own paper. Always before the responsibility had been her teacher's.

As Susie reread for spelling mistakes, she paused to squint at a line, then she reread it several times, voicing the words—behaviors I hadn't seen previously. Her eyes climbed back up the page. They returned to the troublesome spot. Writing posed a dilemma for Susie. She was restless, questioning, dissatisfied. She appeared to be in that state of disequilibrium which sets the stage for problem-finding and problem-solving to occur.

"I did this wrong," Susie said finally, "the whole line." A spelling mistake can be erased, but content revisions mean messing up a paper. Susie was stuck.

Mrs. Howard saw Susie's dilemma. The girl needed a strategy for adding a sentence and more than that, she needed permission to mess up her paper. "It's okay, Susie," Mrs. Howard said, "just draw an arrow and add the sentence."

Thus it was not an elaborate lecture but a light touch which introduced this eight-year-old girl to revision. Mrs. Howard's intervention had been a wise one, it was a response rather than an imposition of information. Because the strategy of adding an arrow and messing up an early draft could be used again in new contexts, Mrs. Howard had provided Susie with a tool rather than simply with a solution to her immediate problem.

Despite the wisdom of Mrs. Howard's intervention, I was discouraged to find that Susie hadn't learned from it—or at least, it didn't seem she had. After circling her spelling mistakes and arrowing in the missing sentence, Susie once again treated her first draft as a final one, working with print as if it were marble, not clay. When she started her next piece of writing, the one which followed her interview with Diane about the bird's nest, there was no indication Susie remembered about messing up the page. Instead, she drew neat margins, and then with tidy letters began a first-and-only draft. I was disappointed, for I wanted good teaching to provide instant results.

When Mrs. Howard saw that Susie had written the general

title, "The Bird's Nest," she and Susie talked about the nest for a minute, and about Susie's interview with Diane. Then, because Mrs. Howard and I had been talking during lunch about helping children focus their topics, Mrs. Howard put her hand on Susie's shoulder and asked, "Susie, what is the one thing your story is about?"

Susie's eyes flickered down onto her title. I imagined she was thinking, "Does she want the story to be about just one thing?" Susie's tight, worried face showed she wasn't sure what was expected of her. Did Mrs. Howard want her to start the story all over, writing just about how Susie's father had helped her learn to fly, since that had been the focus of the interview with Diane? Like most third graders, Susie was eager to please—but in this instance, she didn't know how to. She looked at her title, then began to erase it.

Again Mrs. Howard intervened, and for the third time she tried to show Susie that drafts may be messy. She suggested that Susie scratch out rather than erase. Susie tried to do as suggested. She crossed out the title and beside it, she wrote "Learning to Fly." Then she tried to continue writing her story on the messed-up paper. But when Mrs. Howard left the cluster of desks where Susie worked, I watched Susie solemnly fold the messy page and bring out a clean new one. With careful letters, she began her story again. What a conflict this must have presented to this youngster! Throughout her schooling she'd pleased teachers by being tidy, by doing things right the first time. Could it be that Mrs. Howard actually wanted her writing to be messy?

The episode was a dramatic one. "No wonder children resist revision," I thought as I resigned myself to seeing one draft only.

But although wise and well-timed teaching may not lead to instant results, such interventions leave their mark. In their own time, children surprise us with what they have learned. Susie wrote one careful line on her tidy new piece of paper, and then she muttered, "I'll copy it over tomorrow." As if it had just dawned on her that her paper needn't be a final copy, Susie let her square letters open into a loose scrawl. For the first time, Susie was writing as if there was a tomorrow. (See *Fig. 8.1*, p. 46)

She wrote five or six lines of "Learning to Fly" before Mrs. Howard next reached her side. Again, Mrs. Howard's intervention grew out of our lunchtime discussions. "Susie, do you remember when I did my writing, how I kept on experimenting with different ways to begin my story?"

Susie nodded and I thought back to the day her teacher brought X-rays to school and told the class, "You must interview me." After the class had helped her find her story, Mrs. Howard had

Fig. 8.1

<u>Learning to fly</u>

Once when I was very little I got a hank to fly So I tryed jumping at things and tryed to float up and across I tryed and tryed til my father made me

taken hold of a piece of chalk and clattered letters onto the chalkboard:

My dog fell out of the truck and broke her leg.

Then she had stepped back and looked at her beginning, confessing, "That's sort of a dull lead." She squiggled a line through her words and wrote a second beginning on the chalkboard.

Out of the corner of my eye, I saw Sheba fall from the back of the truck.

"Tell who Sheba is," one child volunteered. With an arrow, Mrs. Howard added the missing information. Soon she'd woven more information into her piece, squeezing details between lines, inserting words into phrases.

Now two weeks later, Mrs. Howard drew a line under Susie's opening sentences, suggesting the youngster try several beginnings and then choose her best. Later we would have called this a "process conference," for Mrs. Howard was not attending to Susie's content or drawing more information from her, but instead she was helping her experiment with strategies for writing and rewriting.

Susie wrote two leads, and then a third. She and her teacher read them together.

1. Once when I was little I tried jumping off things and tried to float up and across.

2. I always wanted to fly but when I tried, I always fell Kaboom! on the ground.

3. Kaboom! That hurt! Why can't I fly? Birds do. Whenever I try, nothing happens.

It did not matter to Mrs. Howard whether the leads got progressively better—she and I cared mostly that the children saw that writing involves choice, that there is more than one way to tell an episode.

I was learning that growth doesn't proceed evenly along an upward trajectory, and so I wasn't surprised when Susie approached her next piece, "Batting Is Fun," as if the first words written onto her page would be the final ones. This time Mrs. Howard was working with other children, but Susie again decided midway that her first draft could be a rough draft. Having relegated neatness to a later stage, she dared to scrawl and even to dot the paper with small corrections. As in her "Lin Su" story, Susie found a major problem among the smaller ones. Whereas in the earlier piece the problem had been missing information, here it was incorrect sequence. Both times, content revisions were prompted by Susie finding an incongruity between her initial text and the event she was describing. Her revisions involved correcting or completing the information—a kind of revision which seemed particularly easy for young writers.

Again Susie was stuck. She wanted to move a paragraph from the end of her "Batting Is Fun" story into the middle of the text, but it didn't occur to her that an arrow could solve this problem as it had the former one. So Susie stood in line for Mrs. Howard's help. Once again, Mrs. Howard showed her how to use the arrow.

This time, something must have clicked for Susie. After this, instead of lining up for help when she wanted to move ideas about on her paper, she invented her own methods. Within a week she was happily crossing out sections and adding arrows and inserting codes into her rough drafts. She independently wrote three rough drafts to "My Dog's Pill" and four to "Batting Is Fun." She not only remembered the lead-writing strategy, she cheerfully wrote seven leads to one story, all without prompting! I was flabbergasted. Mrs. Howard had only worked with Susie on six occasions, and each had been for just a minute or two. Yet the interventions seemed to have set Susie well on the road toward learning the writer's cycle of craft.

Not only Susie, but most of her classmates as well, had already learned these crucial lessons:

1. Most of the children approached a piece of writing knowing there would be a tomorrow. They could relegate concerns about spelling and neatness to a later draft, and in earlier drafts, concentrate on what they wanted to say.

2. Because Susie and her classmates were writing on topics they knew well, many of them had found incongruities between their writing and the events they were attempting to retell. These incongruities led to revision.

3. Susie and most of her classmates had already learned some revision strategies. They knew how to use codes to insert information into the draft; they knew how to use arrows to move a section from one place to another. They

knew how to write successive drafts on a given topic (although the sophistication of the changes between drafts was questionable).

Susie had learned quickly. Clearly, Mrs. Howard's interventions would not have had such an impact on this young learner had Susie not been engaged in her writing. Because she cared about her topics, because she was writing for readers, Susie was an eager learner. But also, the interventions probably gained power because they emerged out of observation, and the timing was right. Still, even considering all that, Susie was learning faster than I could account for. Or so it seemed.

9. Revision?

The leaves had not yet fallen from the trees, and already most of the third graders were revising independently. Like a proud parent, Mrs. Howard brought their leads and drafts to the first-grade classroom and shared them with Mrs. Giacobbe. Back in her own classroom, Mrs. Howard and I marveled at how quickly the youngsters had learned to revise. It was as if eureka had been reached.

Then came the surprising and unsettling news. Mrs. Giacobbe's six-year-olds had taken to revision like fish to water. I was skeptical. Many researchers question whether ten-year-olds can revise; she was telling me revision was easy for first graders?

I hurried down the long corridor to their classroom. Inside the door, an elflike girl sat on the floor with her story spread in front of her. She stapled a flap onto the end of her story and then added more information onto the additional space. When she saw me, the youngster stood up and held her scroll-like story chin high, saying, "My story's as tall as I am!"

At a nearby table, a youngster solemnly alternated between writing and scrunching up her story. She patted the well-worn paper and proudly said, "There, now it's all loved up."

Another youngster had written a book. He turned the pages, saying as he did so, "A robin, a eagle, a parakeet." Then he called to one of his friends, "Hey, Matt, what other kinds of birds are there?" Matt suggested vultures, and the young writer returned to his book to add one more page. While all this was going on, Mrs. Giacobbe was working with another young writer. The two of them had realized that his story, "My Birthday," was out of sequence, and together they were reordering his pages.

Was this revision? I was more skeptical than ever. Revision, as I know it, is audience-aware, reversible; it involves toying with options in the mind, trying things one way and then another. Revision, as I know it, involves shuttling back and forth between writing and reading, between involvement and distance, between looking back and looking forward. I thought of the little girl with her chin-high story. Had she been revising out of concern for audience and clarity, or instead out of the fun of stapling and seeing her story grow? She hadn't seemed to weigh options, but instead merely to add on. She hadn't seemed to view her first draft as tentative, but instead as unfinished. "Her version of revision is certainly not my own," I thought to myself.

And then I realized what I had done. How easy it is to see what children cannot do rather than what they *can* do. Of course, her version of revision was not my own—it was, instead, her own.

Because she was six and I wasn't, her thinking was different from mine. (How clever of me to detect this!) She'd been revising concretely more than abstractly, viewing her draft as nonreversible rather than as reversible. She'd been revising with print as with clay, with blocks, and with bathtub bubbles. Just as revision is a natural part of children's play, it can also be a natural part of their writing.

Only when I define revision as abstract, reversible and as involving an interaction of numerous concerns and strategies might adults have exclusive claim to it. And I thought of Bruner's suggestion that the foundations of any subject may be taught to anybody at any age in some form. "The basic ideas that lie at the heart [of all disciplines] are as simple as they are powerful. It is only when such basic ideas are put in formalized terms . . . that they are out of the reach of the young child" (1963, p. 12).

And what of Susie? I'd naively assumed that behind her drafts, leads and revisions there was a process of thought which was similar to my own. Yet as an eight-year-old, Susie's thinking was probably somewhere in transition between thinking which is bound to activity and thinking which is abstract, between the child's egocentrism and the adolescent's ability to imagine views from many vantage points, between the preschooler's focus on the present tense and the older child's ability to shuttle among various time frames. Not only her thinking but also her revision was probably in transition. As long as I continued to assume that revision meant the same to her as it did to me, I would miss out on her evolving perceptions of it. I returned to my notes and began to scrutinize them, hoping to understand what Susie was and was not doing as she moved from one draft to the next.

What I found was startling. Out of an eagerness to please, Susie had adopted the posture but not necessarily the thinking of a reviser. Whereas once her teachers had prized neatness, now the premium was on messiness. Susie—like so many children—was a pro at learning what is valued. Even in the first-grade classroom, the youngsters had caught on to the new values. One six-year-old said to me, "Mrs. Giacobbe likes good stories and yucky writing. What do you like?" Susie, like this first grader, had learned that revisions were the hot item for the researcher and her teacher. And so, by mid-October she was revising with glee . . . but she had only begun to understand the purposes behind revision.

When I rescrutinized the drafts which had so impressed both Mrs. Howard and me, I found that sometimes the only difference between one draft and the next was the size of the print. Yet Susie chose to write a number of drafts and took great pleasure in recording the draft numbers on top of each page. She sorted her drafts into chronological order at least once a day. When she brought her writing to Mrs. Howard, she was more apt to announce, "This is my fourth draft," than "I've improved my story." The emphasis was on the activity rather than the reason for it.

A baby babbles for the sake of babbling, only later realizing that his voice can be an instrument for communication. A youngster experiments with a typewriter for the fun of pounding on the keys, only later realizing the strings of letters can spell words. "Later" had not yet come for Susie; she was only beginning to learn that revision need not be an end in and of itself, that it could be a tool for larger purposes.

A few of her early revisions had been purposeful. She'd found errors and fixed them, as in "Lin Su," where a line was left out, and "Batting Is Fun," where the sequence was wrong. But the changes had been small ones. They did not affect the voice or framework of the draft. Instead, they worked within the confines of the preexisting draft. I named this common kind of revision "refining." Next to adding on (making stories grow), this may be the simplest kind of revision (Calkins, 1981). In Susie's eyes, most of her revisions fell into this category. When I asked her in early November whether she liked to revise, her answer was, "Yes, if there's a good reason, like it's not neat or you see spelling mistakes or you have the parts mixed up."

As we have already seen, many of Susie's early revisions did involve correcting. Sometimes she corrected surface features in a text, sometimes she corrected incongruities between the text and the subject. But although Susie didn't seem to realize it, in the fall of third grade her more comprehensive revisions tended not to be correcting-revision, as she seemed to think, but instead to be what I call random-drafts. In "Batting Is Fun," for example, Susie corrected the sequence, and changed a few words on her first draft. But then, although she said, "Now I'll recopy this," she did not recopy it. Instead, she tucked the draft under her arm, chatted about baseball with a friend, and then plunged into draft 2 without looking back to the earlier draft and without making deliberate improvements on it. The second draft ended up similar in some ways, different in others. I call this second revision strategy random-drafts because the relationship between the two drafts seemed accidental.

Draft 1

I like to bat because the feel of the ball on the bat makes you proud that you can hit it. But you can't just pick up and hit it if it's your first time. I can now because I practice a lot and after I practice I play baseball with my sister only we don't use a wooden bat . . .

Draft 2

I like to bat because the feel of the ball on the bat makes me feel proud that I can hit it. And one reason I like batting is because it's something you can't do on your first try. I remember the first time I tried and I threw the bat up and when I tried to hit it I just swung around in circles but I practiced and practiced till finally I hit it for the first time . . . But when I play baseball with my sister I hit popflys and I get out but I'm still very proud of my batting.

As the drafts show, although Susie did not deliberately use draft 1 to instruct her as she wrote draft 2, her authority over her subject and her organization increased. By the time she began draft 2, she knew her subject very well, having already written about it once. Through this strategy, Susie gained control of her subject. She did not gain control of her craft. It was by accident rather than by choice that she wrote an entirely new draft 2. She did not compare the drafts once they were both written in order to select the best, and she certainly did not take the best sections from each and combine them into a third draft. I had the feeling she could not have done these operations on her own, had she wanted to. She was riding a wave forward. Her movement between the drafts seemed random, undirected and ongoing.

Oddly enough, this same movement characterized the early form of her third revision strategy, one which I call "listing options." At the start of third grade, the best example of this strategy was when Susie tried different lead sentences for her pieces. I expected that these leads would represent different tacks toward a subject but when I looked closely, I saw that they were only points along a single progression. Each lead was further into the same sequence of events:

Leads
My Dog's Pill
11/6

Every time I come home from school I have to give my dog a pill and it is very very hard.

There now you won't see it. The pill is way down deep in the cookie.

Down it's going, down. Eat it! Oh, no, how am I going to get you to eat it?

Now, today, will you please eat it, for me, the one that feeds you?

Although I call the strategy Susie used here "listing options," the word "options" may be a deceptive one, for it suggests choice and comparison. In the fall of third grade, Susie accurately described her lead writing this way: "I keep on going until I find one I really like." Her movement between leads was an ongoing forward motion—and her products reflected her process.

As I gathered this wealth of details about Susie's writing, I began to see patterns in it. Instead of slotting my information into someone else's schema, I was beginning to build my own.

At first I thought Susie's early revisions could be characterized as belonging to three very different categories. They were either refining, random drafting or listing options. But more recently, I have begun to recognize that each of these forms of revision shared common characteristics.

1. In early third grade, Susie's revisions proceeded along a single track. Rarely did I see her shuttling back and forth between processes. If she was random drafting, she continued to do this throughout an entire draft. If she was refining or correcting a piece, the corrections did not trigger her into a whole new draft. If she was listing leads, she did not stop to reread or revise them nor did she let a good lead proceed naturally into a draft.

2. Susie did not weigh alternatives abstractly. Each sentence which she considered was put onto the paper in front of her, and she only decided against using a sentence after she had written out the entire sentence.

3. Susie operated in the present tense. The content of her writing rarely seemed tentative, for she did not anticipate content changes. Although she sometimes wrote several drafts, while she was writing each draft she tended to consider it as the one-and-only version of the story. Her consciousness did not span several drafts. Instead, in her mind's eye, the first version was replaced by the second, following this pattern:

rather than this one:

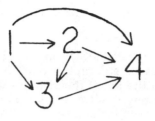

For example, when random drafting, Susie did not reread her earlier draft. She had replaced it; it no longer existed for her. Similarly, when correcting, she corrected something which was wrong . . . and the error was gone. When writing leads, each lead replaced the one before it. Not surprisingly, Susie usually selected the final lead as the beginning of her piece. In none of Susie's early revision strategies was there interaction between options, for such a dialogue would have required Susie's consciousness to span several time/space frames.

10. From writer to reader: Susie develops an executive function

As I gained a picture of Susie's early revision strategies and saw tentative links between them and her thinking, many things began to click for me. Observations I was making as a researcher fit with observations I had made as a teacher; they were combining to form patterns.

Although I remember looking at my generalizations about Susie's early revisions, and being astonished that hundreds of hours of detailed observation had boiled down to three such simple findings, I was at the same time realizing their power was their simplicity. I'd made observations before. What was new for me was that now I could fit flash observations into a larger scheme. Whereas before, learning involved piling more and more notions onto a growing pile of disparate ideas, now the mishmash of ideas was gaining order from a few simple organizing principles.

Although I didn't know it at the time, by characterizing patterns in Susie's writing at the start of third grade, I was preparing myself to recognize changes when they occurred. Unless one sees regularities, it's hard to see irregularities. The presence of patterns provides a ground against which one can see changes. Had I only recorded the flux of Susie's day-to-day behavior, it would have been hard to see changes in her writing. Then, too, it would have been difficult to see changes had I continued to ask only "Is she revising?" I could not easily have plotted movement against a baseline of nos, yeses, and maybes.

In November and December of her third-grade year, Susie's growth in writing seemed to occur primarily in these three areas:
1. Susie developed an executive function.
2. Susie began to internalize concrete physical strategies.
3. Susie developed a wider and more flexible field of concerns.
The first of these changes will be the subject of this chapter. The other two will be the subject of the following chapter.

As a teacher, I used to joke that third graders could do anything except do something in moderation. Once they got going, there was no stopping them. When my children had used exclamation marks, they'd used hundreds of them, developing a hierarchy of fat and thin ones to show gradations in excitement. When they wrote with dialogue, chitchat consumed their stories. When they wrote with detail, they waded through endless minutia. Now, when I realized Susie's revisions also proceeded full force along a single track, all these separate observations clicked into a single pattern.

As a teacher, I'd been exasperated by the way my third graders overdid whatever they did. As a researcher, I could view this phenomenon not as an error, but as a window onto the children's thinking. When I saw that Diane used a steady stream of chitchat in her little stories, I wondered if the reasons she seemed unable to switch out of dialogue were connected to the reasons Susie seemed to lock herself into a single revision strategy. A certain inflexibility is apparent in many of Diane's third-grade pieces:

I wondered if there was a connection between Diane's entrapment in chitchat and Birger's entrapment in sound effects and exclamation marks. These are three of his leads, representative of his writing in early third grade:

1. Wh, Wh, Wh you Brock my tooth Joyanny!

2) kh,kh, Oh, I felt my tooth fall out of my mouth!

3) Slam, Bang, Oh!

In "Learning to Fly," Susie—like Diane and Birger—had seemed to get locked into a single tone of voice, a single perspective in her writing. As I thought about this phenomenon, I realized that Susie's and Diane's and Birger's *products* were similar to their processes. Their reliance on dialogue, their overuse of sound effects, were probably related to the one-track, irreversible thinking of eight-year-olds. So, too, when children's leads follow along a single tangent, when second drafts are sequels rather than revisions, we see symptoms of a kind of thinking which tends to be forward-moving, irreversible.

I was studying developmental theory with new eyes then, asking, "Does this match what I am seeing?" In many instances I was surprised to discover that my hard-earned findings could have been deduced from developmental theories. Bruner, for example, had commented on the one-tracked quality of children's thinking long before I did. In *A Theory of Instruction*, he wrote:

> There is a great distance between the one-tracked mind of the young child and the ten-year-old's ability to deal with an extraordinarily complex world.
>
> Intellectual development is marked by an increasing capacity to deal with several alternatives simultaneously, to tend to several sequences during the same period of time, and to allocate time and attention in a manner appropriate to these multiple demands. (1966, p.6)

Nor was I alone in the recognition that the one-tracked thinking of eight-year-olds affects their writing. Carl Bereiter (1979) emphasized that writers need "a central executive monitor" to shuttle attention back and forth between reading, talking, writing, thinking. Bereiter points out that whereas the nature of conversations allows participants to oscillate between uttering, considering and uttering, the nature of writing is different. Oscillations are not built into the act of writing; they must be supplied by the writer. Whereas Susie had known for a long time how to read, write, question, plan and so forth, what she was less able to do was to shuttle between and to combine these activities.

Flower and Hayes, two other writing process researchers, have suggested that some adult writers also have difficulty shuttling between one operation and another:

> One of the greatest things protocol analysis reveals is that a great part of skill in writing is the ability to monitor and direct one's own composing process. . . .Handling the very process of composing itself is a demanding and, no doubt, learned procedure.
> . . . not all our subjects are able to tell themselves to jot down ideas and connect them later when it would be useful to do so. They seem to lack this degree of conscious control over the process of writing itself. (1980, p. 39)

Now that I saw developmental roots for the lack of flexibility and organization in Susie's early revisions, I expected her strangely pure and deliberate revision to continue through third grade.

Susie began her next piece, "The Big Fish" (November 11th), by writing five leads. While writing the leads her focus seemed to follow the moving tip of her pencil. She rarely paused to reconsider or to plan, and for the most part, the leads proceeded along a single continuum. So far, she met my expectations.

"Hey, Diane, listen to these," Susie said, nudging her friend. As Susie read her leads to Diane, she also read them to herself. The fifth lead went like this, and it was the one Diane paid attention to:

> Our boat was drifting on the water. It was a beautiful warm day. The sun was just going behind some hills and all was peaceful. Just then I felt something on my line. I thought it was a snag but it wasn't.

"How'd it feel like on the line?" Diane asked, a response which was probably modeled after Mrs. Howard's conferences. Children's responses to each other's writing often seemed to be modeled after their teacher's responses. It was not coincidental that some classrooms were filled with commands such as "You should do this," and "Write that," whereas others were filled with questions such as "How did it feel?," "What'd you do next?"

Susie did not answer Diane's question. Instead she ducked her head back toward her paper, reread the lead, and wrote another draft, adding the missing information. When Susie finished, she showed it to me. This is what I saw (alterations are underlined):

Lead 5—Draft 2
Our boat was drifting on the water. It was a beautiful warm day.
The sun was just going down behind some hills. Just then, on my pole
it felt like someone was trying to take the pole (it) away from me.
I thought it was a snag but it wasn't, because it wriggled.

Like Diane, I didn't give suggestions, but even so, I inadver-
tently helped Susie switch from writing to rereading and recon-
sidering. For when she read the lead to me, she found a specific
problem. "How will you know I'm fishing?" she said, not expecting me to answer. She solved the problem by writing another
draft of the lead, then correcting it and recopying it. Now she
was pleased with her introduction to "The Big Fish." "This is
the only time I ever worked on one little section really hard for a
long, long time," she said. "But I got it right."

Lead 5—Draft 1	*Lead 5—Draft 4*
Our boat was drifting on the water. It was a beautiful warm day. The sun was just going down.	Me and my father were fishing at a lake. I looked in the water and saw a quick flash. It was a school of fish that looked like silver dollars.

Her fourth version of the lead shows little semblance to the
first one, but what is more important, there were deliberate
reasons for the differences. Revision, in this instance, did not
involve an arbitrary forward motion, nor was it bound to following a single recipe for revision. Instead, Susie has alternated between random drafting, writing, reading, correcting, recopying
and talking. In all, it had taken her 287 written words and eigh-
teen revision codes (cross-outs, arrows, stars, insert codes) to
build a beginning which satisfied her. And it had taken a great
many shifts between processes.

Susie continued to rework "The Big Fish" with revisions we
will look at more closely later. For now it is enough to say the girl
continued to defy my expectations. What had happened? No
sooner had I decided that the one-tracked quality of her early
revisions was developmental, than her writing began to weave its
way among many processes. What had brought about such sudden changes? Had her development been turned to fast-forward?

The question sounds like a joke, yet without jesting, I answer:
Yes. Yes, her development had been switched to fast-forward,
something which would happen time and again for many of the
children in our study. Over the next year-and-a-half, they would
continually surprise me by pushing beyond their "developmental level." In doing so, they not only showed me the kind of
changes in writing which we might expect of older children, they

also reminded me time and again that the presence of developmental characterisitics does not mean we carry within us a blueprint for growth in writing. Teaching—in the richest sense of the word—interacts with development and changes it. Teaching can be the cutting edge for learning, as Vygotsky stresses in this passage:

> What the child can do in cooperation today he can do alone tomorrow. Therefore the only good kind of instruction is that which marches ahead of development and leads it; it must be aimed not so much at the ripe as at the ripening functions . . . Instruction usually precedes development. (1962, pp. 101, 104)

Instruction does not necessarily come from a teacher. In "The Big Fish" episode, Diane and I had both unknowingly been instructors. By listening to Susie's work-in-process, we had encouraged her to listen to it herself. Our presence had helped provide Susie with a "central executive monitor" (Bereiter).

It was turning out that the workshop hum in Mrs. Howard's classroom was important in ways none of us had anticipated. Mrs. Howard had encouraged children to share their work while it was in draft form because she knew sharing could provide motivation; it could keep the plates spinning. Now we were finding that audiences also provided another important function, for even when children said nothing at all in response to each other's pieces, their mere presence as an audience during writing dislodged writers from their one-tracked adding on.

Now when I work as a consultant in schools, teachers often approach me with worry, asking, "How do I guarantee that my children are being helpful to each other in their child:child conferences?" The worried teachers and I sometimes talk about the importance of being models for good conferences, and often I stress that children are more apt to model their conferences after their teachers if we are consistent in our conference tactics. Sometimes the teachers and I brainstorm ways to improve child:child conferences. But always I tell teachers they can relax. Even if a child says nothing at all in response to the piece of writing, it is crucially important for young writers to have listeners throughout the drafting process rather than simply when the piece is finished. Even if audiences simply listen and retell what they hear, they will have given writers a chance to reread their own stories. In doing so, the audiences have dislodged writers from simply adding on. The presence of a listener encourages writers to become readers of their own emerging texts. In even very simple peer conferences, children provide each other with an external executive function.

In time, if children have easy access to real audiences, they will internalize the audience. As we will see, Susie soon asks herself the questions which have been asked of her by her friend and her teacher. She grows to anticipate her readers' need for detail and appreciation for action. She learns to take into account that her classmates need background information. But perhaps more basic than all of this, she internalizes the executive function. She learns to switch easily back and forth, from the role of writer to reader, from using the hand to using the eye, from moving forward to sensing backward. And as Sondra Perl says so well, this oscillation is a crucial part of the writing process:

> Composing does not occur in a straight-forward linear fashion. The process is one of accumulating discrete words or phrases down on paper and then working from these bits to reflect upon, structure, and then further develop what one means to say. It can be thought of as a kind of "retrospective structuring"; movement forward occurs only after one has reached back, which in turn occurs only after one has some sense of where one wants to go. (1979, p. 18)

11. Sequences in Susie's writing development

My research was beginning to resemble the process of writing a novel. "It begins with a character," Faulkner says, "and once he stands up on his feet and begins to move, all I do is trot along behind him with paper and pencil, trying to keep up." It was certainly all I could do to keep up with my main character, for Susie was changing quickly.

Children's growth in writing, I was discovering, isn't all that different from their growth in math. In both disciplines, the learner moves from a dependence on overt physical actions toward an ability to mentally reproduce operations. Whereas at first children solve the problem $15 \div 3$ by taking fifteen unifix cubes in hand and sharing them out among three people, soon the children invent shortcuts and symbolic representations. Instead of getting out their cubes, they form mental pictures of them and the sharing-out happens in their mind's eye.

Piaget has shown that such a move, from overt physical actions to mental actions, is typical for the middle childhood youngster. He describes the move, saying, "Internalization means that the child does not have to go about his problem solving any longer by overt trial and error, but can actually carry out trial and error in his head."

Internalization is a key concept for me in my study of Susie's and her classmates' growth as writers. Often over the two years I found that new operations entered Susie's writing process as concrete, systematic behaviors. For example, when she first deliberated over topic choice, she elaborately listed ten topics, then used stars of various sizes and numbers to rank the topics. Once she had selected one item from this list, Susie broke it down into subtopics, which she listed alongside the item. Finally she underlined one subtopic and it became her topic. Within a few months, she had internalized these steps and chose topics while looking up at the ceiling or chewing her pencil. "I'm going to try writing about . . . " she'd say. She would no longer rely on writing them down; she could consider alternatives in her head.

A similar pattern characterized the changes in Susie's lead writing. When she first considered several possible leads, she did this through a stylized procedure of listing numbers 1 to 5 down the margin of her paper, then writing a possible beginning alongside of each. She wrote each lead out in full, and separated them from each other by a careful line. This was the procedure she followed in order to get her lead to "The Big Fish."

Later in that episode, however, Susie used the lead-writing strategy to tackle a new problem, and while doing so, she short-cut the procedure. After completing her first draft of "The Big Fish," Susie reread it. "I want to make the section where I catch the fish shorter; it should be quicker," she said. She sighed, cast her eyes about the classroom, reread the piece several times, sighed again. These were all familiar signs that she was restless, and I knew this could mean she was ready to make a break-through. I suspected Susie was wrestling with the logistics of how to fix a section which was embedded in the middle of a piece.

No one came to Susie's rescue, and so she decided, quite independently, to adapt the lead-writing strategy to meet her new problem. On a separate bit of paper, she listed numbers 1 to 3 as if she were writing leads. Beside both the numbers 1 and 2, Susie tried alternate ways of writing the section from the middle of her piece. Then she circled number 3. She was ready to try again. For a few minutes her pencil was still. Then she brought it to the paper, held it there, ready to write. She pulled away.

I asked, "What'd you almost write?"

Susie blushed, "I was going to say, 'Just then a quick jerk awakened me and I looked and saw my pole bending,'" she said, "but it was too long." Now she was quiet again, her pencil dabbing occasionally at number 3 and her lips moving as she whispered more alternatives to herself. For the first time that I had seen, she was internally considering optional ways of saying something.

It's significant to notice that by listing numbers 1 to 3 in her margin, writing leads beside two of the numbers and pointing at the third, Susie had built a concrete scaffolding within which she could organize the flux of alternate leads which crossed her mind. It seemed each time she considered an option, her pencil dabbed at number 3. Bruner gives a similar example of the way in which a concrete operation can provide children with an internalized structure within which to operate. He says:

> In the example of the balance scale, the structure is a serial order of weights that the child has in mind . . . Such internal structures are of the essence: they are the internalized symbolic systems by which the child represents the world. (1963, pp. 36, 37)

"I might try thinking back to the time and remembering what I really did," Susie said after a while, and then she rewrote the section again. But still she was not pleased. "I don't like how it fits with the rest of the story," she said, and once again she was revising. Susie later described the process this way: "I was thinking of what really happened and what would fit with the real thing and look good on paper."

As the year continued, lead writing, like topic choice, eventually became an internalized process. As this table illustrates, Susie eventually considered possible leads without putting more than a word or two onto the paper.

Number of Words Susie Writes Before
Finding the Lead Sentence She Uses

Date	Title	Number of Words
9/18	Clockmaker	0
9/21	Lin Su	0
10/9	Kaboom	91
10/16	Batting	0
10/23	Surprise in Canada	258
10/25	My Dog's Pill	163
11/27	The Big Fish	287
1/5	Saturday Nights	192
1/15	Snuggling	266
3/1	Birthday Teddy Bear	46
3/14	Washing Caspar	14
3/20	Pop-wheels	10

Flower and Hayes (1980, p. 42) have suggested that not only for children, but for writers of all ages, growth in writing is often marked by an increasing ability to depend on procedures which have become automatic and routine. By developing memory schema for certain kinds of writing and certain writing processes, writers are able to focus their attention on new, and increasingly complex, aspects of writing. This is what I saw happening for Susie.

When lead writing and topic choice became internalized, it did not mean Susie's entire writing process moved underground and became invisible. New problems were tackled, new considerations entered into her writing, and they occupied the place once filled by lead writing. A pattern emerged: something entered as a concrete operation, later it became internalized, making room for Susie to deal concretely with something new. In a sense, it can be said that what entered as revision later became "pre-vision."

It was not only the movement and the concreteness of Susie's writing process which were changing, it was also the dimensions of her field of concerns. In September, Susie focused on the moving tip of her pencil. The questions she asked related to the word at hand: Is this right? What should I say in the next line? She did not seem to move from this local, text-bound level of concern to a more global one, something which Flower and Hayes suggest is common also in the adult basic writer (1982, p. 321).

But by late November, this had begun to change. Susie's consciousness spanned a wider time-frame and took into account a greater variety of factors. During "The Big Fish" episode Susie reached back into the past, deliberately trying to bring it to bear on her thinking. She strained to recall details of the fishing trip, saying "I'm thinking back to what I really, really did then." She looked back not only to past events, but also to past drafts. Once she wrote a new draft, she no longer totally dismissed the old drafts. While writing "The Big Fish," Susie also reached forward in time, anticipating both future drafts and a future audience. "Will they know what I mean?" she asked. The time dimensions of her writing process seemed to be expanding in new and important ways.

Finally, the dimensions of Susie's fields of concerns were also expanding because she had a growing awareness of the qualities of good writing and a new ability to consider several of these simultaneously. As I reported in an earlier article (Calkins, 1981), her choices now emerged from "tension—between writing for information and writing for grace, between inclusion and focus, between intended and discovered meaning."

She said, for example:

> I'm having a problem putting all the stuff that happened into the paper. I could write a big, big book on it, and I want to put just a tiny bit . . . deciding what tiny bit to put down!
>
> I was thinking of what really happened and what would fit with the real thing and look good on paper.

As she wrote, one concern vied against another. She wanted to provide her audience with needed information while still making her story action-packed; she wanted to make her piece true-to-life while still maintaining her focus. As a result, she shuttled between focusing on the text and the subject, between attending to language and attending to information. The dimensions of her field of concern went from this:

language and attending to information. The dimensions of her field of concern went from this:

information (what to say next?)

convention (is this right?)

to this:

information (what to say next?)

convention (is this right?)

action (it has a lot of action. I like when it goes plop!)

focus (it tells a lot about just one thing)

tone (I want this part to be shorter, quicker!)

organization (I don't know how this fits together)

sequence (what happened next?)

truth (I want to think back to what really, really happened . . . have it fit with the real thing)

audience (will they know where I am?)

ending (I don't know if the ending is too good)

feelings (it tells the exciting parts)

detail (putting all the stuff that happened . . . I could write a big, big book on it)

Susie's new concerns probably came from the changed environment in her classroom. Because she had real audiences, she anticipated future readers. Because she wrote on true topics, she could recreate the events as she put them on paper. Because she was learning her friends liked action and sound effects, Susie wanted to include these in her story. Because she had seen classmates cutting and pasting their papers in order to put sections into the right order, she was aware that sequence is something writers think about.

Although Mrs. Howard did not sit children down and teach them about "qualities of good writing," she helped the children become aware of what works in a piece of writing. Susie's attention to focus, details, sequence and so forth grew out of the classroom context. But her ability to weigh one concern against another simultaneously may have related more to her development than to instruction. I do not know, but I suspect that no classroom environment could lead a six-year-old to maintain such a wide field of concerns. First graders tend to consider qualities of good writing singly or serially (Newkirk, 1982). Also, their attention tends to be more closely bound to the here-and-now, to the word-at-hand. Although they may write for an audience, often that audience does not extend beyond their classmates. Often they do not imagine a future time when their story will exist without them. When Mrs. Giacobbe urged six-year-old Amy to add missing information to her story by asking Amy how her readers would know the information if it wasn't included in the text, Amy's response showed her inability to envision a distant and separate audience. "Simple," she said, "I'll invite them to my birthday party and tell them." In time, some first graders *do* add information to their texts so as to answer an audience's questions. But for many, the ability to write for a distant and separate audience comes later.

Alex, another six-year-old, showed a typical first-grade focus on the present tense. When he picked up his pencil to write, I asked, "What will your story be about?" Alex seemed dumbfounded by the stupidity of my question. "How should I know, I haven't drawed it yet," he replied. Again, some first graders show a greater ability to plan ahead; there are exceptions to the generalization that first graders tend to focus on the here-and-now. But on the whole, the nature of a first grader's perception of good writing tends to be quite different from that which Susie showed in "The Big Fish," and certainly the extent to which first graders can simultaneously juxtapose one concern against another is different. Like both the executive function and internalization, the child's field of concerns probably relates to cognitive development as well as to teaching and to experience with writing.

12. The life-story of one text

When I unbraid the threads of Susie's writing development and follow each one separately, I risk losing sight of the larger fabric. In doing so, I lose many of the advantages of the case-study approach. In this chapter, therefore, I will not analyze Susie's writing progress during the next portion of third grade; instead I will show it. The chapter contains an episode in Susie's writing development as it happened within the larger drama of classroom life. Readers will see each aspect of writing which I have emphasized thus far interacting within the chapter:

1. ownership
2. pace and control of one's pace
3. writing conferences
4. Susie's executive function and the role dialogue plays in it
5. Susie's field of concern and the way she makes one concern vie with another
6. internalization
7. Mrs. Howard's role in each of these

Newfallen snow made my trip from the University of New Hampshire to Atkinson School a slippery one, and so I arrived late on the morning of January 7th. The children were already gathered in a meeting to share their writing. Their eyes watched Susie, for it was her turn to share. "This is my final draft of 'Saturday Nights with My Father,'" Susie said, which surprised me because I knew she'd only begun the piece when she returned from Christmas vacation two days before. I wondered what had happened to her notion of revising until it was her best, but I did not have long to ponder the question for my thoughts were interrupted by Mrs. Howard, reminding the children to listen well. The room grew quiet and Susie began to read:

I love Saturday nights when my father lays down with me.

Then she proceeded to tell about watching TV together and how they get hungry and her father heads for the kitchen:

I know what he's going to make—his famous spaghetti with homemade sauce. Then when he takes a big plate and a little plate, I know I am going to have some too.

The story continued, describing every step of their Saturday night ritual.

When Susie had finished reading, a scattering of children raised their hands. Because it was Susie's text which was being discussed, she was the leader of the meeting. She called on Renee. "I like it, it's really good," Renee said. Then catching a glimpse of Mrs. Howard, she tried to be more specific, saying, "I like it because you put your feelings down." Assent rippled through the group, and Susie blushed. There were other compliments and each was specific: "You told about just one thing," "You had lots of details like about the plates," "You put it in order."

Then Jeremy responded in a different way, asking, "What part did you like best?" Jeremy's unusual contribution did not go unnoticed, for much of Mrs. Howard's teaching consisted of helping children notice and see the significance of what they did. A month earlier she'd called attention to a child who gave a specific rather than a general comment, and now Renee and the others remembered to give specific feedback. On this January morning, Mrs. Howard called the class's attention to Jeremy's question and they talked about the significance of helping each other look back and evaluate their own work. A group was formed to collect a list of questions which children might ask to help each other look back and reflect on their own texts. Meanwhile, Susie was thinking about Jeremy's question.

"I like the part about snuggling with my father," she said, and six more hands shot up; new interests, new comments, perhaps new questions.

Again Mrs. Howard intervened, for she wanted the children to follow through on each other's questions, to view a question as the beginning of a probe. She asked Jeremy if he could respond to Susie's answer, and so he asked, "Why is that your favorite part?"

Soon Susie was describing snuggling with her father in great detail, telling about piling pillows on her daddy's feet to keep them warm and how sometimes they would wrap themselves in a puffy quilt. "Sometimes my sister snuggles with us, too," she said. "That's the best of all, cause then we get to go on our parents' king-sized bed."

The story was a touching one, told with such simplicity and warmth that several classmates responded in unison, "You should write about that!" And so Susie decided her next piece would be "bumped off" from the previous one, and she would call it "Snuggling with My Father."

Because the next day was Thursday, the class did not have

writing workshop. Instead the children worked in their now streamlined Language Arts Skills program. Only the few skills which had not been integrated into either the writing or the reading programs were still being taught in isolation. Although Thursday was not a day for writing, Susie told me she'd been thinking about her story.

Susie didn't know it, but she was not the only one who'd been thinking about her story. At lunch, teachers had heard Mrs. Howard's rendition of Susie's tale and the young girl and her father were fast winning their way into the hearts of everyone.

When the children came into the classroom on Friday morning, their daily writing folders lay waiting on their desks. It was Craig's job to come in early from recess and pass out the folders so that writing workshop could begin smoothly when the children reached their desks. Today, however, Mrs. Howard broke the precedent by asking the children to gather on the rug for a brief preliminary meeting. The children knew what was expected of them in these meetings since the rules by now were implicit:

1. Only bring your writing if you want to share it.
2. If you have papers with you, lay them on the floor in front of you.
3. Do not bring pencils to the meeting.
4. Listen well.

At this particular meeting, Mrs. Howard asked the children in the circle to each tell what they intended to do that day. As usual, the children were at many different stages:

"I'm brainstorming for topics."

"I'm copying my final draft over into cursive."

"I have five leads on "Waterslide" and I need a conference to help me choose the best one."

"I'm just getting down information on bats. My writing is going to be a report."

Because a number of children were choosing topics, Mrs. Howard suggested they stay at the rug for a meeting while the other children dispersed. Susie, Birger, Craig, Diane and Amy— the five children I was following the most closely—returned to their cluster of desks in the back of the room. For a few minutes, the room was filled with a hum of activity as twenty-six children sorted through their writing folders and chatted about their plans. Soon Birger and Amy went off to the rug for a conference, and the other youngsters in our cluster settled into their own work.

My chair was pulled close to Susie's and I was curious. I'd been perplexed by her abbreviated process in "Saturday Nights with My Father." What would she show me today? Had her sustained process in writing "The Big Fish" been a fluke, an isolated event? Now as I sat with clipboard in hand, I wondered if I would see her executive function at work, organizing a variety of processes. Would I see her shuttling back and forth among a number of concerns? The process of research, like the process of reading a good book, had caught hold of me and I couldn't wait to read the next line.

Susie wrote a 1 on her blank sheet of yellow paper. She held her pencil beside the number and looked up. She glanced around the room; then her eyes flickered back toward the paper, then again around the room. At first I didn't know it, but she was writing leads.

"I thought about some," Susie said a moment later, "but they are not right. I'm trying to think how it really happens: how does Daddy get on the couch and how do I get there?" Professional writers have said that the hardest thing about writing fiction is getting a person from here to there—I was surprised to see an eight-year-old struggling with the same problem. "Usually I'm in the den and then he lugs wood for a while," she said to no one in particular. "Then he takes a shower and we wait, and when the shower is over, he comes out and stretches and then lies down . . . " Her voice trailed off as momentum shifted from mouth to hand and she was writing:

1. Bang! There goes the hamper. He must be almost done with his shower. I can't wait. "Jill, make room, Dad's coming."
"No, I will when he gets here."
"Well, here he comes, Hi, Daddy!" My father motions with his arm to push down, but I am already.

Susie stopped, skipped a line and wrote 2. Had she progressed immediately into her second lead, I suspect it would have been a continuation of the first. The product would have reflected the process. Instead, Susie distanced herself from her text by showing it to Diane. They read the lead together, and Susie asked, "Do you have any idea how I could start my next one? I gotta think of a new one." Although she hadn't said a word, Diane had already played her part. Susie did not even wait for a response. She just reread her lead and started thinking of how she could change it into a better beginning. "I might leave out the first part of that lead and start it, 'I can't wait, Jill, make room.'" She wrote a second lead, adapted from the first, and now Susie reread both and said, "I thought the first was good, but I think this one is even better and now I'm going to keep on, and I may take parts from each one. But after my Dad takes a shower, my Mother does, and she wears a flowered robe. But I don't think that's important to my story."

The allotted forty-five minutes for writing had passed, and Susie knew it was almost time for the share meeting which marked the end of each writing workshop. She wrote her third lead quickly, again adapting it from the first. The noise level in the room picked up as meeting time drew near. Papers were refiled into folders, conferences were brought to a speedy close, and at 12 o'clock the children were in place, seated cross-legged in a circle, waiting for the much enjoyed ritual of watching Mrs. Howard hold her hip, sigh, and climb onto the floor with them. In all her years of teaching, this was the first time she had considered the floor as usable space and it came more naturally to the children and me than to her.

Twenty-six children waited. Although perhaps a third had papers on the floor in front of them signifying that they wanted to share, only four or five would be called upon today for each piece deserved some response and the meetings never exceeded twenty minutes. Susie was the third to share. As was the custom, she began by saying where she was in the writing process and what kind of help she needed. "I've just written three leads," she said, "and I want to know which sounds best to you."

   1. Bang! There goes the hamper. He must be almost done with his shower. I can't wait! "Jill, make room, Daddy's coming out! . . ."
   2. I can't wait. "Jill, make room, Dad is coming out of the shower," "Noooo, Susan Sible, I will when he comes out!" "Well, here he comes, hi Daddy!"
   3. "I can't wait," I said, jumping on the couch. "Jill, make room, Daddy's coming out of the shower . . ."

Susie's classmates liked her third lead, but Susie didn't. The next writing workshop began with Susie writing a fourth lead. When she finished it, she sought feedback from Wendy, one of the best writers in the room. Wendy listened to the new lead:

   4. My father came in from hauling wood. "Daddy," I asked, "will you lay down with Jill and me?"
   "After I fill the wood stove up and take a shower . . ."

"Can't you make it longer, just putting it all down?" Wendy asked. When Susie looked quizzical, Wendy tried to be more specific. "You could add sentences between each sentence. Like in the lead, 'My father came in from hauling wood,' you could add, 'He had sawdust in his hair,' between the two sentences. You could put in another sentence and it would give more feelings to the story."

I was stunned by Wendy's insight, for she was right. Susie rarely "built up" her pieces with those "sentences in between." Each line of Susie's pieces furthered her sequence of action—

she wrote with vertical rather than horizontal sentences, and for now, this quality sometimes resulted in a scantiness in her stories.

But Susie just shrugged and said she guessed she'd have to do it her own way. Rather than repairing her fourth lead, she started over again on a new sheet of paper, which may have helped her approach the subject from a new tack. This lead had a different tone:

> I snuggled deeper in the blanket. I felt uneasy. Something big was missing and I knew what it was. It's Daddy, I think, and he's in the shower. I hear the water click off. "Whoopie! He's almost done and then he can lie down . . ."

Without talking to anyone, Susie reread the lead and drew slashes through several parts, then carved out the one section which she liked. She wrote it on another bit of paper.

> I snuggled deeper in the blanket. Something big was missing and I knew what it was.

"Now, what I have to figure out is how, with the same feeling, can I bring my father to the sofa," Susie said. She wrote numbers 1 through 3 at the bottom of her page, as if she were about to list possible leads, but instead she listed possible ways to maneuver her father onto the couch. None of them "fit" and so Susie decided that the final line in her original section didn't connect with anything. She crossed it out, and one cross-out led to another. Soon Susie was shaping her words as if they were clay. (See *Fig. 12.1*, p. 74)

Susie was getting closer now and she knew it. She worked silently, as if afraid to break the spell. Selecting what was good from her draft, Susie recopied it and again reshaped and refined her words. Finally, she successfully maneuvered her father to the sofa, and the section was complete. She read it aloud, proud of her efforts. (See *Fig. 12.2*, p. 75)

With black ink and an italic pen, Susie copied "Snuggling with My Father" for a final time, then pasted the little piece onto page seven of a slim, homemade book which held her finished work. Then the girl took a huge stack of papers from her Daily Writing Folder and began to sort and label the rough drafts which comprised the real history of "Snuggling with My Father." She tucked the pile of rough drafts into an already bulging Cumulative Writing Folder, then whispered to her friend, "Hey, Di, look how fat this folder is getting." Giggling, the two girls pretended the folder was too heavy to lift from the table. "All that work," Susie said happily, "for seven tiny pages!"

"Same with my writing," Diane said. "Like at home—we have to get about a million buckets of sap before we get the tiniest bit of maple syrup."

Fig. 12.1

I snuggled deeper in the blanket
I felt uneasy. Somthing big was missing
and I knew what it was
The feeling of missing something
that made me feel
empty It was bigger than a

Then Somthing I needed because
I was sad and it would cheer
me up. I felt lonty without it. But
Its not missing any more here comes
Daddy!

than and

Its my father
I must be daddy I think
I look around the room to
make sure nothing else is
missing and the only thing
thast missing is daddy!

Fig. 12.2

> I snuggle deeper in the blanket.
> I feel uneasy. Something big is missing.
> Then, Daddy comes in and lays down with
> me. He makes a pocket with his legs.
> I crawl in.
>   I feel happy I do not have a lonely
> feeling anymore.

But to Pat Howard, the final pieces sometimes didn't seem like Grade A syrup. Without jesting, she would groan, "All that work—for this." Then I would remind Pat that she wasn't teaching pieces of writing, but young writers. No matter what the final pieces were like, none of the drafts, none of the experiments, were a waste, for each left a mark on the writer, if not always on the writing. I didn't necessarily believe what I was saying, I was mostly trying to cheer her up. Only now, as I pore over the data, does it occur to me that I was right.

Whereas Susie's revision during the first half of third grade often entailed writing alternative leads, by the time she finished her snuggling story, Susie seemed to have internalized the process of considering alternative beginnings. Instead of following the elaborate procedure of listing leads, Susie just jotted down a word or two, thought, looked around the room, thought some more, and then began her story. What was once revision had now become pre-vision. What was once an elaborate, long process, now happened in the jotting down of a word or two, or in a moment's pause.

Each time Susie wrestled with a writing dilemma, it was as if she added a new layer to what she could bring to later writing episodes. She was growing like an onion—deeper, with more internal layers.

It's easy to misread the importance of this, as I did. I remember watching Susie internalize revision behaviors, and thinking, "This will save her time, but things won't be fundamentally different." But abstract thinking *is* fundamentally different from physical activity, as I soon began to realize.

13. Between the lines: Susie's process becomes internalized

I wonder if ever a school sent and received more Valentine letters than Atkinson Elementary School did that year. The writing bug had spread, not by decree but by contagion, from child to child, from grade to grade, until even the teachers were writing. "I think we saw how much fun the kids were having and started getting jealous," one teacher told me.

A writing support group had formed with a cluster of teachers meeting twice a month to share their writing, and on Tuesday mornings eight of us had begun holding breakfast meetings to exchange ideas on teaching writing. I did a lot of listening at those meeting—and so did both Mrs. Howard and Mrs. Currier, who would become Susie's fourth-grade teacher. Afterward, Mrs. Howard would come to me and say something like, "You know—that idea of Janet's seemed really good—do you think I should try it?" Invariably I'd say yes, and soon she became more confident in her own ideas and stopped asking.

And so for me and for the third graders in room 209, those winter mornings began to hold little nutshells of surprises. At the start of a writing workshop—or sometimes midway into it—Mrs. Howard would often say to the children, "Would you all gather on the rug," and then she'd have a mini-lesson. "I'm trying to add something new to the classroom pot," she explained to me. "I know these little lessons won't meet each child's needs but they're only five minutes long, so I don't worry. I know they'll work for some kids, and for others they'll just be exposure."

In one meeting, she asked children to compile a list of Do's and Don'ts for selecting a good topic. Soon this list was hanging on their bulletin board:

Do	Don't
Do write about something you care about.	Don't write about things that are boring to you.
Do start off with action, with the here-and-now.	Don't write about something you haven't done yet.
Do choose just one aspect or part of your topic.	Don't keep going if it gets worse and worse.
	Don't pick a topic that's too big for you to be detailed.

In another meeting, Mrs. Howard suggested that each child read aloud the lead paragraph from his or her reading book. Then the children discussed the way some leads involved action and dialogue, and others were flashbacks:

The Trumpet of the Swan by E. B. White

Walking back to camp through the swamp, Sam wondered whether to tell his father what he had seen.

"I know one thing," he said to himself, "I'm going back to that little pond again tomorrow."

The Midnight Fox by Betsy Byars

Sometimes at night when the rain is beating against the windows of my room, I think about that summer on the farm. It has been five years, but when I close my eyes I am once again by the creek watching the black fox come leaping over the green, green grass.

To help children focus their pieces, Mrs. Howard sometimes asked them to find or to write one sentence which conveyed the essence of their story. Similarly, sometimes she suggested that the children listen to each other's writing or to literature and try to capture the writer's main idea, the thread of the story.

A natural extension of this work on focus were the mini-lessons on mapping. When children wrote reports—whether on assigned topics or on their own individual interests and projects—they tended to mix together everything they knew, as Brad has done in his piece, "Tennis."

I know a lot about tennis. I know that when you play you should get a good quality racket, such as one from Wilson, Spaulding or Head. When you play you should also play at a time either early in the morning or late in the afternoon, because at twelve o'clock to four thirty it is very hot playing. Tennis takes lots of practice. I usually play tennis at least one and a half hours, and it really is fun, but it's hard work. My favorite tennis players are John McEnroe and Chris Everett Lloyd. They are really good.

Some of the things you have to do to be really good is mainly to practice. The other things you must do are to practice certain shots, such as: forehand, backhand, lob and serves.

If you don't practice these shots on a regular basis you won't be good enough to play in competition. When I grow up I would like to play at Wimbledon or the U.S. open.

In a mini-lesson, Mrs. Howard would help children like Brad to map out their information on a topic. Brad's map might look like this:

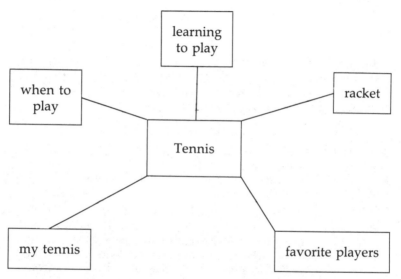

After making such a map, Mrs. Howard would suggest to the class that Brad could consider treating each subtopic separately, perhaps in a separate chapter or paragraph.

Although often Mrs. Howard's mini-lessons dealt with concepts which were familiar to her class—such as leads, focus, telling detail and rewriting strategies—she also began to share with her children the concepts she was gleaning from books such as Murray's *A Writer Teaches Writing* and Zinsser's *On Writing Well*. In several lessons, for example, she asked children to find places in their writing where they'd *told* the reader something. Then she would help the writers show rather than tell. Murray describes the concept of "show not tell" this way:

> You may tell us "it was hot." Or you may show us by writing, "My shirt stuck to my back. Sweat ran into my glasses." In the first sentence, we had to take your word for the heat. In the other two sentences, *we were there*. We too have the same stickings and sweatings. Showing makes it possible for the reader to identify with the writer. (p. 228)

In February and early March, Susie's responses to these meetings puzzled me. She'd listen attentively, or so it seemed, but when she returned to her work, none of the new concepts seemed to stay with her. In retrospect, I think I understand. It was as if Susie were saying, "My head is full; I can't take in new things until I can manage what I've got."

Just as when baby mice are given a smorgasbord of foods, they instinctively eat a balanced diet, Susie was being no less wise. As soon as she could, she began to take in the new notions—slowly, one at a time, reminding me of recipes which say, "Add flour slowly, stirring all the while." And so the next months of Susie's writing development can be described as a time for mastery, and as we will see in the next chapter, for new revision strategies and for a growing awareness of components of good writing.

Mastery didn't come in the shape one might have expected. Susie did not grow more articulate, more in control of her pieces, more logical. Instead, the opposite happened. She grew less articulate about what she was doing and why, and her writing became less a matter of deliberate control. Although I didn't realize it at the time, Susie was growing toward a mastery which wasn't the school kind of mastery at all, but instead the mastery of a craftsperson.

The first signs I saw of this change came on a springlike morning in early March. I sat with clipboard in hand waiting for Susie to begin a story about the teddy bear she'd been given when she was "going on eight." I expected Susie to list—or at least, to consider—possible leads. I'd grown accustomed to her step-by-step progression through the writing process. But instead of exerting her usual systematic control over the creation of a story, Susie surprised me by saying, "I'll write this draft and it will tell me where to start it."

The draft would *tell her* where to begin! I felt the shock of recognition, of hearing my own experience put into words, and thought of others who'd spoken of this sense. Samuel Butler once said, "Do not hunt for subjects, let them choose you, not you them. Only do that which insists upon being done and runs right up against you . . . "

The sculptor Henry Moore described a similar feeling. "I sometimes begin a drawing with no preconceived problem to solve, with only the desire to use pencil on paper and make lines, tones and shapes with no conscious aim; but as my mind takes in what is so produced a point arrives where some idea becomes conscious and crystallizes, and then a control and ordering begins to take place."

Susie's writing about her teddy bear reminded me of the early stages in Moore's sculpting. "I was writing like wildfire, just going after whatever came to me," she said. Susie had made a few revisions, but this time the additions and deletions were not the focus of her attention. They were, instead, a tool. Whereas Susie had once approached writing as a linear system of activities which she imposed upon herself, now her writing process had loosened its bondage to this systematic sequence of activities and she was able to "write like wildfire," going after whatever came to her. The writing process was no longer the goal in and of itself. It had become more amorphous, more playful, more intuitive. The resulting story was perhaps the most coherent, unified piece of writing she'd done that year:

The Wonderful Birthday Present

My sister handed me a big box. "Open it!" She cried. I did and, in the box was a big ball of fur with eyes! HAPPY BIRTH-DAY!! Shouted my parents.

I took the fur out of the box and it was a big brown teddy bear! I stared at it. It was so perfect with a big yellow bow around its neck. It had big brow eyes. "Do you like it?" Jill asked. "I love it thank you."

That night I slept with the bear. Its soft fur felt warm and cozy. I never knew how nice it could be to sleep with. Before I would have felt uncomfortable. But I cant imagine not sleeping with my bear now.

It would be easy to lean back in the rocking chair and say, "Susie has internalized much of the writing process, and this internalization means she can focus better on her subject." This is probably true but the label 'internalization' seems inadequate because it doesn't convey the freedom and power Susie has gained. Besides, internalization suggests a single phenomenon, whereas changes had actually happened on many different levels.

On one level there was the fact that Susie's drafts looked very different. In early third grade, her pages reflected a deliberate and steady process, and no wonder, for every turn and step of her revision had been grounded in physical actions. Although Susie could vary the pace of those actions somewhat, her revisions had been held back by the fact that they were bound to activities. In early third grade, Susie couldn't flash forward in her mind's eye to consider the implications of a new word or an altered phrase. Her thinking couldn't zoom ahead to see where a tangent might lead. Because each consideration was written out in full, Susie's pages in third grade tended to reflect an even-keeled, steadily increasing energy, as in these examples of her third-grade work:

The Big Fish

by: Susie Sible

→ Me and my father were fishing at a lake. I looked in the water and saw a quick flash. It was a school of fish that looked like silver dollars. I saw a few long pieces of grass but to my surprise they were little fish! Suddenly I shouted dad I've got a fish!!! Dad what do I do? Try to reel it in, nice and slow. I tryed but it was too hard. Boy was he big.

→ I thought maybe if I pull him up into the boat it will be easier. But before my father could stop me I pulled the fish close enough to touch him and just then PLOP!!! the fish fell out into the water. I was sad. My father explained to me, that you can't pull it up out of the water. After that I did n't fell so bad.

I was going on a trip in canada and we were taking are camper and I was excided. because I herd abaut all the wild aniomals tha whit was scared but Jill hoped to see them. told When we started going I asked my father just what kind of anrimals we might see? He said deer Arey other ones I asked oh He said maybe bear

(2) Wheee! Where on are way to canada! I never thight we woold relly get to go but we did and think of all the things we will see Strems going down montans fish dear oh I cant wait to get There And we almost are

(3) When we were in caneda at a camping grand I decided to help...

By early fourth grade, things were different. Susie was nine and a half years old and far more experienced as a writer. When revising, she needed only to touch base with concrete activities and strategies. It was typical for her to list several numbers and then simply to point to each number as she weighed alternatives in her mind. Many times I'd watch her put a single word onto a paper and then look up as if the written word had set into motion a chain of thinking. Often she'd reread a draft and simply underline the sections which she wanted to "spread out with more detail." Then she would proceed to write an expanded draft. Because her revision process was becoming more abstract, her pace could become more varied. Sometimes her drafts mirrored an easy, loping process like this:

① They must
be telling me
about what they
were talking out
I want to

DRAFT 2

Ⓐ Downstairs I heard my mother
and sister talking. They say things like "Oh No!"
Or "Poor Caspar." I walked over to the over
way where I could hear them better. was I
didn't know what they were talking about
but when I heard "Poor Caspar" I knew
something must be wrong with my dog Caspar.
I stood silent and still listening.
I listened carefully to see if I could
find out what was wrong. Then I heard
my mother say "Don't tell Susie about
this." After I heard that I just be My
heart starting beating fast.
● Maybe Caspar got hit by a car and
got killed. I ran downstairs. I had to
see what was wrong with Caspar

Others, like these, reflected tautness, conflict and thinking
which sped ahead, then turned back on itself:

> My mother told me to ~~I started crying again~~ sit down
> and rest ~~to see if things~~ then she looked at my
> head ~~I~~ + was O.K ~~E I am~~
> ~~am glad there was a~~
> cushion were my head hit
>
> Draft 2
>
> . Plop!!! I opened my
> eyes ~~and looked around~~ What
> happened. My ~~head hurt~~ #
> ~~I started crying~~ My mother
> ~~walked over and asked~~ I
> was ok I guess I said.
>
> → ~~I I~~ was shocked ~~out~~
> ~~the My~~ father came back
> ⊕ I aced all over. Next time
> ~~I would I will never~~
> sleep on ~~the~~ top I don't think

In the cross-outs, arrows and inserts, one could see traces of her thinking.

Other changes were also becoming evident. It's significant that in early third grade Susie had written out each of her sentences in full and followed each tack to its logical conclusion. Her leads had not trailed off, her drafts had rarely been discarded midstream, and her sentences had been written out before they were evaluated and possibly discarded. A year later, in early fourth grade, things were different. Susie's drafts often contained scraps and pieces of ideas juxtaposed against each other. For example, in the story about a moped ride with her father, Susie wrote the letters *I fe*, then crossed them out and wrote *we*, then crossed it out. When Susie finished the piece, I asked her about the cross-outs. Susie explained, "When I put down 'I fe', I was wondering if I should do a little more about how I felt, or should I put more about tightening my grip and speeding down the hill. Then when I put 'we', I was thinking whether I should make us approach the house or not."

"How do you decide?" I asked.

Susie thought for a moment. "I think how it would sound.

Either I put it down or I just think it, and if it doesn't sound right, I think of a different way."

How quickly things had changed! Only months earlier, I'd noticed Susie's attention was bound to the word at hand, to the moving tip of her pencil. Her drafts had consisted of a methodic, linear sequence of activity. Now five letters, crossed out, represented a whole chain of thought, a dialectic of free association and critical thinking. By early fourth grade, when Susie worked with print, she also worked with potential print. Her attention was continually looping ahead, then pulling back, creating an interaction of ideas and time-frames. There was no longer a separation between writing and revision. As Susie drafted, she also revised. The two happened simultaneously. Her drafts had become anticipations of more drafts. No longer did Susie view her revisions as once-and-for-all corrections.

What this means is that Susie's thinking had gradually freed itself from a reliance on the word at hand, and also from the activity at hand. She not only anticipated the ends of sentences begun, the conclusions of tangents started on . . . she also anticipated her own writing process. Now her writing involved not only present-tense concerns, but also the future tense and the past tense. She could zoom ahead in her mind's eye, and she could turn backwards. This new time-frame made profound differences in Susie's writing. While in third grade, revision tended to be a·way to correct errors, by early fourth grade it had become a way to experiment. While in third grade revision usually involved a backward movement to correct or replace something "wrong," by early fourth grade revision involved a new sense of possibility, of exploration.

The differences between Susie's comments about her writing in third grade and in fourth grade illustrate well the new playfulness which had entered Susie's revisions, the new willingness to loosen control and to follow wherever her craft and subject led:

Early Third Grade	*Fourth Grade*
I did this wrong, the whole line. —"Lin Su" story, September, third grade.	I like this draft, but I might be able to do it better; I'll see.— "Falling out of the Bunk," September, fourth grade.
Shouldn't I have put this part about the pop-balls up ahead where I write about playing baseball with my sister?— "Batting Is Fun," October, third grade.	I'll try it out and read it over, see what it says.—"Falling out of the Bunk," September, fourth grade.

I don't think I should have the word 'back' two times in a sentence.—"Surprise in Canada," October, third grade.

I don't like this lead because you wouldn't even know I was talking to my dog.—"Dog's Pill," November, third grade.

How will they know I'm fishing . . . I better put it in. And I want to make this section shorter, it should be quicker.— "The Big Fish," November, third grade.

I don't know if the ending is too, too good or not. It might be boring.—"The Big Fish," November, third grade.

I'm going to work around in here, writing and changing.—"Flying in a Jet," October, fourth grade.

I'm just going to try another draft, or another part of the story, or start it differently.—"Around the Campfire," January, fourth grade.

I can't think of anything to fix up in the draft so I'll put it away and write a whole new draft and see. When I write the new one, I might find out there are parts I don't like from this one. Even without thinking about it, I leave them out.—"Quiet and Peaceful," April, fourth grade.

What I want to do next is to add detail . . . I'll take the details from these drafts and fit them together. No, no, I'll just work on a draft 7 and make it fresh. If it turns out, I'll stay on it. Otherwise, I'll go back and take from the others.—"A Wonderful Walk," April, fourth grade.

When I asked Susie in early third grade if she liked to revise, her answer had been, "Yes, if there's a good reason. Like it's not neat or if you see spelling mistakes or you have the parts mixed up," but in fourth grade her answers were quite different. She said, "Yes, you can mess it up, you can do anything you want to do." Then she added, "Usually I put down a sentence that isn't the one I like. It isn't even in the piece. I just put it down and I can go right through it." Susie paused. "After I write so many drafts, I read them over and take parts. There is a special feeling about them."

Because by fourth grade, Susie anticipated learning through writing, she wrote with a new tentativeness, like an artist at a sketch pad. When she finished a piece, even her evaluations were tentative. "I don't know if I like it; I gotta go and see," she said, and "It might be good; I'm not sure."

Another telling sign of Susie's new tentativeness was the fact that, for the first time, she chose titles after the piece was done rather than before she'd started it. I asked her why and Susie answered, "How could I write my title first—I don't know what the story will turn out like, not 'till I write it."

The tentativeness created a need for new codes. Susie invented "light cross-outs." These tiny pencil lines meant "This might have to come out; I'm not sure." And instead of using scissors to cut her stories into separate pieces, Susie began to use dark dividing lines at the end of a section. "I make believe these are scissor cuts," she said. "I can just erase the lines if I decide it's all one story—it's easier than pasting the pieces back together."

The new flexibility in the time and space dimensions of Susie's writing process meant that she had taken a significant step forward. No longer did Susie consider each draft, at the moment of conception, as the one-and-only version of a story. No longer did each draft replace the one before it. For the first time, Susie was able to move between several alternatives, interacting with her options to create new possibilities.

And so, by fourth grade, we have new words to describe Susie's writing process: tentative, anticipatory, flexible, interactive, responsive. Onto this list I want to add one more word: embodied. Whereas in early third grade, Susie's writing seemed to be a product of her mind alone, now it was as if Susie's knowledge about writing had left the realm of her mind and moved into her hands, her eyes and her ears. She would often preface her revisions with "This part sounds like something's wrong," or "These don't fit together," or "My biggest problem is how to tell people what they need to know and still have it sound right." Whereas before her judgments had been logical and articulate, now it was as if, in her hands she could feel the shape of her piece, and in her ears she could listen for connection and flow and pace.

Visitors to the classroom would watch Susie and her classmates as they wrote and say they had a magic touch. They would marvel that Susie could pick up a pencil and with hardly a false start, write pieces which began like these:

I peeked into the tunnel. Cool air struck my face. I stepped in, and the cool air was all around me. "Wow," I said softly. My voice echoed.

I stopped and rubbed my sore legs. I squished my toes into the small puddles that were in my sneakers, and looked down from the mountain. I felt good—like I had really accomplished something by climbing that mountain.

"Susie is gifted," the visitors said, and I agreed. Gifted with the courage and the skills to experiment with writing. Gifted with the human potential to learn through trial and error.

The writing abilities of the children in this classroom were quite remarkable. Yet there had been nothing remarkable about their growth as writers. Susie's skills had not appeared full-blown out of nowhere nor had those of her classmates. Instead, the skills developed step-by-step, the way all learning happens. Susie's magic touch was not the result of a miracle but of experience and good teaching. She was not born with a talent for writing. She'd developed that talent through working at her craft. She'd gained a skill through the process of doing her best and then making her best better.

To me, it wasn't surprising that by fourth grade Susie could easily produce good leads, focus her story and use telling details. These were things she'd worked on. Of course, there were many aspects of writing she hadn't yet worked on, and in these areas, she was still self-conscious, deliberate and concrete. But no wonder. In these areas, she was still just learning.

14. Longer stories and bigger revisions

Fourth grade brought many changes. Susie had—quite literally—grown under my eyes. The pixielike eight-year-old was now nine, gangly with four inches of new height and shy about her braces, glasses and early adolescent pimples. Gone were the old references to snuggling with her daddy. Now Susie tended to write about her sister, her mother, and, most of all, her friends. She wrote about a puppet show she and Diane performed for their parents. She wrote about trying to fry bananas, and about the day her dog escaped. And a new form of writing entered her repertoire: love-notes. "Alan loves you," she'd write, then crumple the note into a wad and pass it from her desk to Amy's.

Susie's interests weren't the only things which were growing up. Her penmanship, too, was changing from uneven, lopsided printed letters to even, careful cursive ones.:

Third grade:

> that most of the crumbs of pill were in her mouth and then I let her outside. Oh No is it going to be the same way to tomorrow ?!?!

Fourth grade:

> It was a nice night. The sky was full of stars. I wanted to go outside so I decided to join my sister Jill while she emptied the garbage. When I got out on the grass I started playing around. I was doing cart wheels and summer saults when I heard a nell. "SKUNK!"

Despite her cautious penmanship, Susie's pieces had doubled in length. In third grade, most of her drafts were less than a page long. In fourth grade, they usually exceeded two pages; and they were not only longer pieces, there were also more of them. Susie had written about a dozen final drafts in third grade, but she wrote three times that many in fourth grade.

Susie's new facility with writing, combined with growing confidence, led to more daring revision strategies. Now as Susie got her hands onto a draft and began to mold and shape it, she worked with bigger units. Over the course of fourth grade, she developed and internalized several strategies for large-scale revisions. These are the subject of this chapter.

The first in a series of large-scale revisions occurred on a crisp October morning, one year after Susie was introduced to the concept of leads by having her teacher draw a dark line underneath Susie's opening sentences in "Learning to Fly." This time, Susie independently wrote and revised two drafts of "Flying in a Jet Plane," sharing the story occasionally with her friends but not with Mrs. Currier, her teacher. Now she reread the second draft:

> We found our seats and sat down. "We're really on a jet plane," I said. I just couldn't sit still, I wiggled around in my seat. I reached over to hold my mother's hand. "This is kind of scary," I thought. I looked out the window. I thought it might be better if we could have flown in the daytime. "I think we're moving," I said. We were moving backwards. A little truck was pushing us. It pushed us to the runway. Then we started again, going slowly, then faster, and faster. I was pushed against my seat. My stomach felt hollow from the speed. I looked outside. The runway lights were going by faster and faster. The wheels were rumbling on the ground. All of a sudden, everything was smooth. "We're flying."
>
> I stared out the window. The higher we go, the prettier the lights looked, all different colors in funny patterns. I was so glad we were flying at night. I felt so excited.

Susie looked at the page for a few minutes, her eyes flickering from the beginning to the end of it. She seemed restless, and so I knew that I should stay near. "There is only one thing about the whole story," Susie said finally, her forehead creased into deep think-lines. "I don't know if I should cross out the whole first half and start if by making myself up in the air, looking down." Susie was hesitant, but nevertheless drawn to the idea. Penciling a dark line across her page, Susie said, "This is instead of cutting it up. I'll read it first with the early section; then I'll read it without that part. I'll see which is better." She had invented one of her first tentative revision-codes, the dividing line. Soon Susie decided that the pencil line could become a more permanent move. She scratched out the front half of her story:

For a long time it had seemed that Susie knew her writing could be made stronger and denser by eliminating extra sentences and words, but not until fourth grade did she regularly consider eliminating whole sections from her pieces. Susie seemed to have learned what Picasso once said:

> In each destroying of a beautiful discovery, the artist does not really suppress it, but rather transforms it, condenses it, makes it more substantial.

I recently showed the crossed-out section of a "Flying in a Jet Plane" draft—and those from other drafts—to Professor Leaska of New York University. An expert on Virginia Woolf, Leaska has spent years studying rough manuscripts of writers' work. He was astounded at Susie's page. "Letting go is the hardest thing for writers," he said, and then showed me how writers usually make hesitant, small cross-outs. Leaska wanted to know what had prompted Susie to make such bold, definitive cross-outs. I did not know the answer.

After Susie cropped "Flying in a Jet Plane," she refined and enlarged the remaining section, building it into an entire story. Like a photographer in a darkroom, this young writer moved between cutting and expanding. These are the changes that result:

Sections of Draft 2

We found our seats and sat down . . . I wiggled around . . . I looked out the window . . . A little truck was pushing us. It pushed us to the runway. Then we started very slowly. We started again, going slowly, then faster and faster. I was pushed against my seat. My stomach felt hollow from the speed. I looked outside. The runway lights were going by faster and faster. The wheels were rumbling on the ground. All of a sudden everything was smooth. "We're flying."

I stared out the window. The higher we got, the prettier the lights got. All different colors in funny patterns. I was glad we were flying at night. I felt so excited.

Final Draft

We started going slowly, then faster and faster! It was so fast I was pushed against my seat. I looked outside. The runway lights were going by very fast. The plane wheels were rumbling on the ground. All of a sudden, everything was smooth. 'We're flying!' I said.

I stared out the window. The higher we got, the prettier the lights looked. They were all different colors in strange patterns. I was so glad we were flying at night. I was so excited.

Right under us, I saw a big, dark hole. "What's that?" I asked my mother.

"It's the Boston Harbor," my mother said. The moon made a light on it. I could see the water now. I saw a long strip of lights; they were cars on the road. Everything looks so different when you fly.

After a while I felt tired. Over our heads was a little cabinet. My mother got a pillow from inside it. I lay down with the pillow under my head. Soon I was fast asleep.

Susie was pleased with the improvement in her story, but in retrospect, I sense that her strategies for large-scale revisions were not yet a natural part of her writing process. After Susie wrote a first draft of her next piece, "Seeing My Grandparents," she changed only words and sentences. Then she recopied the draft, again making small changes. Because it was a good story and Susie had invested herself in it, Mrs. Currier decided to intervene in a way which might challenge Susie. "Do you notice that all of your stories seem to be about the same length?" she asked. It was a wise observation, for Susie seemed to have developed a tendency to write two-page stories, and each story was similar to the next. In the discussion that ensued, Susie's teacher suggested that the girl challenge herself by taking the two-page draft of "Seeing My Grandparents" and extending it into a six-page draft.

This was not a common interaction between teacher and student—but it proved to be an effective one. Susie came to the writing session the next day, eager to meet the new challenge. "I decided at home how to do it," she confided in me and then she began rereading the two-page draft, circling sections of it with her pencil. "These circled parts are places I can spread out with more detail," she explained. Susie was approaching this new challenge as she approached most new things—in a systematic deliberate way.

Susie's first decision was that she could tell more about arriving at the airport—so that section was circled. And she could tell more about the crowds of people waiting at the airport—so that section was circled. "I had no idea there were so many parts I could fix up!" she said, her voice high with excitement. "I'm discovering more on this draft than I ever did. I never realized I could change so much!"

Watching Susie's eager response to Mrs. Currier's challenge, I was reminded that in the Piagetian growth model, organisms do not just grow on their own. They grow in response to interactions which challenge them, interactions which dislodge one equilibrium so that a new one can be reached. One of the tasks of a writing teacher is to intervene—with sensitivity and with a sense of timing—so as to nudge children toward new discoveries.

By the time Susie finished circling the sections of her draft which could be expanded, she had circled most of the page. Then she set to work, recopying a few sections and expanding others. Let us look at the differences and the similarities between the circled draft and the final one:

Draft 1—with circles	Final Draft
I started walking up to the airport from the plane. We had to go through a tunnel. I squeezed my mother's hand.	My mother and I started to get off of the plane. My sister, Jill, was right behind us. I looked at Jill. Her face was red from

I couldn't wait to see my grandparents.

excitement. She smiled at me. I giggled. I could tell she was just as excited as I was.

By pulling my mother's hand, I hurried her to the entrance of the airport. As we got nearer, I heard the crowd inside, laughing and talking. I saw a lot of people. They were looking for the person they came to meet. They stretched their necks, searching through the crowd. Everyone was smiling, everyone was happy.

We were almost in the end. I saw my grandparents.

My grandmother's face was tanned. It made her look so healthy. My grandfather looked pretty much the same except he was tanned too. Somebody stepped in front of me. I lost sight of my grandparents. The crowd was moving very slowly so I wiggled past everybody. I ran straight to my grandparents. First I went to my grandmother. I threw my arms around her.

I ran to my grandmother and just hugged her. We were both so happy to see each other. My grandmother laughed and cried at the same time.

"Hi, Babydoll!" My grandmother said. I gave her a kiss. My grandmother's eyes were filled with tears but she was laughing. We were so happy.

I let go of her and ran to my grandfather's arm. "Hi Bubba," I said.

I turned around, my mother was hugging my grandfather. Jill was, too. I ran to him. He saw me and laughed. I hugged him, "I missed you both a lot," I said.

"I missed you and Jill," he said.

"Hi, Susie," he said. After we finished saying hello, we went to get our luggage.

I just couldn't believe I was with my grandparents in Florida. It had not struck me what time it was until I looked at the clock: 2:15 in the morning! Wow! I didn't realize how tired I was.

I thought of my father at home. We promised to call him as soon as we could. I wondered what he was doing right now.

"Susie," somebody said. It was my mother. "We have to get our luggage now," she said. I took hold of my grandparents' hands and started off.

Although I didn't know it at the time, Susie had developed a strategy which would become important not only in her own writing, but also in her classmates' writing. As she usually did when a child invented a new strategy or worked in a new mode, Mrs. Currier asked Susie to tell the class about her revisions.

A day or two later, I watched Birger rereading a draft entitled "The Day My Cat Died." I asked Birger what he was thinking about as he reread the story, and the Norwegian boy answered, "I'm trying to make parts longer, like Susie did in her piece." Birger continued, "I'm going to add on at this part, when I come out of the garage, to the cat's accident. I'll tell about when I was walking across the driveway and I heard sounds, like the vet with the siren, and I smelled the air." Birger paused for a moment, and then, in his matter-of-fact way, he continued, "It wasn't bad air. I remember thinking it was hard to think that a part of me had just died—the air was so nice and clean." Then he said, "I'm going to add on that into the circled part" and he set to work.

Before long, Susie and her classmates were using the circle-and-expand strategy in conjunction with the dividing line strategy. On a cold December morning, Susie came into the classroom, bursting to tell her friends about the skunk that had been caught in their garbage can. When writing time came, she confided to me, "After it happened my sister and I were riding in the car and I made up a little story to my sister. I pretended I was an author and told her, like, 'Once upon a time, there was a young girl who went out to the garbage can . . . '" Then Susie began to spill words onto the paper, writing in quick, loopy letters. When she finished the draft, she shook out her cramped hand. It had been an unusually long story.

Draft 1

One night I accompanied my sister to empty the garbage. She started emptying the garbage while I was playing on the lawn. All of a sudden I heard a shriek. "Skunk!" someone yelled. My sister ran by. I started screaming, too. I didn't see the skunk but I still screamed. I ran to the house.

My father didn't know what was wrong. "A skunk!," we were crying. But later on me and my father went out to investigate. We started walking to the garbage can. I was hiding behind my father just in case he started to spray my father would block me. As we got closer I stayed behind. But after a while I went up to my father. He flashed the flashlight around the garbage can. "Where is it?" he asked.

"I think I heard Jill say *in* the garbage can."

"*In* the garbage can?" he asked.

We went closer and looked in the garbage can. I didn't see anything, but my father said, "He's there."

We decided he was trapped in there, but how to get him out?

My sister started creeping slowly behind. I was still hidden behind my father. I asked my father to pick me up so I could see the skunk. He did. I looked in and saw two glittering eyes. The skunk looked exactly like the ones in the zoo.

While I was in my father's arms, he started walking towards the garbage can for a better look. I jumped down. I did not want to go any closer.

"I know how to get it out," I said. "The big stick that holds the clothesline up will work."

"That's a good idea," my father said, "we'll try it."

My father told me to open our screen porch door so when he tips the garbage can he can run before the skunk sprays.

"Ready?" my father asked.

"Yes," I said.

With a brave attempt my father tipped the garbage can and came running to the house as fast as he could go. When he got to the house, we all looked out to see if we could see the skunk running off. Nothing happened. After a couple of minutes, a little skunk came trotting out of the garbage can as calmly as ever.

We went in the house and told my mother what had happened. There was one question: how did the skunk get trapped in the garbage can with the lid on?

My father didn't do it. I didn't do it. Jill didn't do it. We all looked at my mother. "Did you put the lid on the garbage can recently?" we asked.

"Yes, I did," my mother said, not knowing what she had done. "Mom!" I yelled. "You put the lid on while the skunk was in there!"

As Susie scanned her first draft, she fixed up small parts of it. This combination of writing and refining by now seemed to be a natural part of Susie's writing process. It was surprising to me that Susie still perfected word choices, smoothed over transitions and added descriptions to her first drafts, for often she later discarded these drafts. It was almost as if these small touch-ups helped her gain distance on the piece.

Because I'd grown accustomed to the rhythms of Susie's writing process, I was not surprised when the next day Susie announced, "I'm going to do a whole 'nother draft." Before she began, she reread draft 2, circling several sections, and then halfway through the story she drew a dividing line. "I might take off the whole end of it," she said, using the strategy she'd invented a month earlier during the "Seeing My Grandparents" story. Soon Susie had expanded the first part of her draft and cut away the rest. Now her story began with emptying the garbage can and ended with the two girls yelling, "Skunk!" Susie was pleased with this new version, but her friends were not.

Instead of reading the condensed version of her skunk story to one child in a conference, Susie met with four youngsters in what was called "a writers' circle." The procedure in these circles was that one by one, each of the four children took a turn reading his or her piece out loud to the others. Mrs. Currier, like Susie's third-grade teacher, Mrs. Howard, emphasized the importance of writers reading their pieces aloud. Both teachers believed, as Peter Elbow says so well in *Writing with Power*, that "there is a deep and essential relationship between writing and the speaking voice." Elbow elaborates, "To write with clarity and power requires an essential act of taking full responsibility for your words—not hedging, holding back, being ambivalent. Reading your words out loud is a vivid outward act that amplifies your sensation of responsibility for your words."

And so Susie had read her shortened skunk piece out loud and explained to her friends what she'd done to it. They insisted on hearing the original version as well. After comparing both, Diane said, "I don't know if you're going to agree, but Suz, the ending of the first one was good! You should keep the whole thing."

When the writers' circle was over, Susie quite happily erased her dividing line and set to work again. Her efforts proved productive, as is evident in the differences between selected sections of draft 1 and comparable sections in her final draft:

Sections of Draft 1

I was playing on the lawn. All of a sudden, I heard a shriek. "Skunk!" someone yelled. My sister ran by. I started screaming too.

The Revised Versions of These Sections

I was doing cartwheels and somersaults when I heard a yell. "Skunk!!!" Jill was running to the house as fast as she could run, still screaming. I knew she saw a skunk. All of a sudden, the night seemed very scary. The dark shadows of big trees crept over the yard. I did not want to be out there with a skunk, so I ran right behind her as fast as I could.

We went closer and looked in the garbage can. I didn't see anything but my father said, "He's there." We decided he was trapped in there, but how to get him out. I asked my father to pick me up so I could see the skunk. He did. I looked in, two glittering eyes looked up. The skunk looked exactly like the ones in the zoo.

My father very slowly walked closer. He shone the flashlight in the garbage can. "He's there," my father said. I was too short to see the skunk over the garbage can so I asked my father to lift me up. He did. I looked inside and there he was. It was a small skunk. It had a small head compared to the size of its body. The flashlight made its eyes glitter. I was still looking at the skunk when my father started walking closer with me still up in his arms. I did not want to get any closer to the skunk so I jumped down quickly.

Over the course of the two-year study, there were many instances such as this one in which Susie adapted a revision strategy to meet new needs. We have seen how in her third-grade writing workshops, Susie used the lead-writing strategy first to determine where in the sequence of events she could start her story. Then, in "Snuggling with My Father," she used it to experiment with different approaches to a subject. In "The Big Fish," when she wanted to revise a section which was embedded in the middle of her piece, she adapted the lead-writing strategy to this new situation by listing numbers down her page and writing alternative ways to phrase the section. By the end of third grade, Susie used the strategy in yet another way, for now she often considered alternative leads in her mind's eye, and adapted the lead-writing strategy to meet a new challenge: thinking up possible endings and titles for her pieces.

In third grade the lead-writing strategy was particularly important. In fourth grade it was the circle-and-expand strategy which became an integral part of many of Susie's revisions, adapted to meet her changing purposes. At first she used it as a way to expand on key sections of "Seeing My Grandparents." Later in that same piece, Susie used the strategy to evaluate whether the piece worked. "I'm going to reread it and think about it as sections; how I like each section. I know there are certain sections I like better than others and I wonder if I can do anything about it." As she picked up the story, she muttered, "First the part about when we entered the airport." Her eyes scanned the section. "I like it a lot. In this part I learned to describe people more and to add little things like 'we giggled'." Susie's eyes moved down the paper. "The next section is about the crowd." She drew lines, framing the section. Knowing Susie, I was not surprised to see that when she divided the piece into parts and worked on each part separately, she did it with pencil in hand, in a systematic and concrete way. It would not have been enough for her mentally to divide the piece into sections. She needed to draw lines, to ground the new way of thinking in physical, hands-on activities.

When Susie reread the section, she said, "It's kind of a long section and there are certain parts of it I like better than the others." She took a new sheet of paper, explaining to me that it wasn't for a whole new draft, but for a new draft of just that section.

Susie's next adaptation of this circle-and-expand strategy came in February of fourth grade. This time she was not writing a personal narrative, but instead, a social studies report. Probably because Susie was used to viewing a piece as a collection of sections, she was intrigued with the way reference books were divided by subtitles. She decided to do the same to her report on the Valley Glacier. And so Susie squeezed onto Diane's chair, and the two best friends talked about their reports. "I'm thinking of adding little subtitles," Susie told Diane, and showed her one of the reference books. "See, it's still all one main thing, but subtitles." A few minutes later the two girls came up to me and asked, "When you make subtitles, can you just say anything you want?" Soon Susie had inserted headings into her report:

The Beginning of a Glacier
Making Mountains
How They Melt
Studying the Glaciers
What the Glaciers Left Behind

Susie's next step came when she was working on "Swinging Vines," a story about an amusement park ride she and her mother had been on in Florida. Neither draft 1 nor 2 impressed me, but I wondered what Susie thought of them. "Susie," I asked, "what's the difference between the drafts?"

Susie's reply startled me. "Draft 1 begins in this order: discussion of the ride, then description, then discussion." Glancing at the second paper, she said, "In draft 2, the order is the opposite. First there's description, then discussion." Susie chatted along as if it was the most natural thing in the world to conceive of one's own text in terms of these subtle changes in tone. "On this draft, I started right *on* the ride," she said, reading the opening line to me: "The ride was going its fastest . . ." She continued, "But on the next draft, I tried to ease it into the describing, not just to jump into it." To show me the difference between what she called "easing" and "jumping" into description, Susie compared these two versions:

Jumping	Easing
The ride was going its fastest.	The ride was going its fastest.
I was at Bush Gardens in Florida.	I was on the ride at Bush Gardens in Florida.

I looked at the two drafts and could sense the difference she was telling me about. But where had she learned to categorize and analyze the sentences in her pieces?

On her next story, Susie again made an easy, offhand reference to the various effects of different sections of her text, and again I was amazed. She said, "In this 'Around the Campfire' story, I notice that up here I have a different tone, explaining, than down here." It seemed that these new developments had come out of thin air. To me they represented a sudden leap forward in Susie's ability to distance herself from her own work and to view it analytically in terms of both what she was saying and how she was saying it.

But now, as I reflect back on Susie's development as a writer, the changes seem less surprising. I can see where the groundwork had been laid. In fourth grade, as earlier in third grade, revision strategies which entered as concrete, systematic and self-conscious routines had once again ceased to be elaborate rituals and become part of Susie's "felt sense." Instead of occupying her focal attention, these strategies were tools which she could use toward other ends. It had become natural and easy for Susie to divide her texts into sections in order to analyze each section. What had once involved systematic, conscious control was now part of her "magic touch." Once again, Susie had gained control in order to lose it. She'd become conscious of revision strategies in order to become unconscious of them.

Throughout much of third grade, the focus of both Susie's attention and mine had been on her activities during writing. But in time, I was able to observe her writing without concentrating my attention on her developing ability to revise. What I saw was that Susie had also begun to put other concerns onto center stage.

The remaining sections of this book will deal with these new areas of interest. None of them are totally new, for they were all implicit in my discussion of Susie's growth during third grade. What will be new is the attention I want to pay to these topics.

In the next six chapters, I will introduce Susie's new classroom and her fourth-grade teacher, Mrs. Currier. We have already read some of Susie's writing during fourth grade in the last two chapters, but we need to look at the changes in her classroom. So we will move back briefly to the transition between Mrs. Howard and Mrs. Currier. Then my emphasis, like Mrs. Currier's, will be on conferences. After this there is a chapter in which I will discuss Susie's concept development, followed by chapters which involve reading, writing and Susie's work on a social studies report. And then, finally, I want to consider again my theme, "Lessons from a Child."

III.

The Writing Classroom: a context for growth

Peter Micha

15. When teachers collaborate: new ideas

Sometimes, especially toward the end of the year, Mrs. Currier would slip hesitantly into room 209, the third-grade classroom. Cautious not to intrude, she'd hover on the edges of the room, her quiet blue eyes taking in the activity of Pat Howard's writing workshop. "I have so much to learn," she'd tell me. Often she brought a spiral notebook with her and she'd take notes on all she saw. She never stayed long. I'd see her glance at the clock and then slip away, off to do just one more thing to prepare for her class' return from gym.

If Carolyn Currier came into the teachers' room, it was only to fix herself a cup of tea and then to leave as quietly as she'd entered. She was always busy with the children: writing little notes to them, searching the library to find a book for a specific youngster, reminding the boys to zip their jackets or they'd catch cold.

By May of that year, I realized I wasn't intruding if I visited in her classroom during lunch. And so we began spending time together. I went to her room hoping to talk about the year ahead, but somehow it seemed more important to hear about her grandchildren and to talk about my newly acquired stepdaughter. "Just love her," Carolyn advised me, "and keep on loving her. Give her time and she'll come around."

May turned into June and suddenly the school year was ending. Carolyn became busier than ever with her students, and I, with my research. There hadn't been time for us to talk about the year ahead. I was glad when Carolyn asked Pat and me if we could get together for breakfast some Saturday.

Her house was as I suspected—a little Cape with a white picket fence. A basketball hoop hung from the garage. "Lyman put it up for the neighborhood kids and for the grandchildren, when they're older," Carolyn explained as she walked with us toward the house.

The kitchen smelled of freshly baked muffins and of coffee, still percolating. Pat and I were effusive in our thanks, but Carolyn insisted *she* was the one to be grateful. "Thank you for taking the time," she said, and opened her spiral notebook to a new page.

Pat, full of her usual energy, admired every nook and cranny of the house, exclaiming over each of the framed pictures. Only then did she join us in the dining room. "Let's make an agenda," she suggested.

"If it is okay, could the children be first on the agenda?" Carolyn asked. "I want to hear about the ones I'll be getting."

Pat needed no urging. Soon the three of us were poring over the cumulative writing folders which Pat "happened to bring along."

Carolyn knew Craig from the playground, and so we brought out his first and his final pieces from third grade:

I was Divnin the seRwoLand asan
to caRS cRashrgan I anstcRoshing Rot into.
trcmB ut I tuRnedoway and than I Turned
Satout To get away and and then 5 moRe caRS
cRasheing ght beh t neam ect scaR cmg

The Battle of Slippers

I was walking up the hall, not expecting what was going to happen to me. Boom Boom. I was being attacked by my brother, Steven. He was throwing slippers at me.

I yelled "help." I ran down the hall into the kitchen. I heard my mother yell "Steven and Greg stop throwing slippers." But we did not stop throwing slippers.

I went up to Steven to tell him we had to make some rules. He said "you're right."

One rule he said is just throw the slippers underhand. Then he said and no turning on lights. I said "oh darn." I was mad because I could not turn on the lights so I could not see him as good.

I hid beside my mother's bed. I saw Steven come in the room. Boom Boom. I fired at Steven but I failed to hit him. He

it me in the stomach, ow" I said
I ran down the hall and lay down
on the couch. Then I noticed that I had no
slippers. I walked up the hall to tell Steven I had
slippers. Then I said, "Steven, I have no slippers."
But it was too late zoom zoom. Steven was
bombing me, then he picked up a slipper and
started to hit Steven.
I was hiding under Steven's bed.
Steven walked up the hall. He looked in my
room, started to laugh. He heard me. Then I
laughed some more. He knew I was under his bed.
Back! He hit me in the face.
Then I crawled out from under the bed.
Whack, whack. I got hit again in the head
ow" I yelled.
I jumped on Steven. He picked me up from my
legs and put me down head first. While he was
picking me up, I said "this is no fair." He said,
"Why not? Because 75 pounds to 124 pounds is
just not fair."
Steven was up my my, hitting my on the bed. I had
no slippers but I saw one. I reached for it. I
got it. I hit Steven in the head. Then I heard my
mother say, "come and eat."
I said, "thank god."

The End

Not every child had improved as much as Craig had. We'd been perplexed, for example, to see Diane's confidence and skills disintegrate over the course of the year. We brought out one of Diane's first pieces, written concurrently with Susie's "Lin Su" book. Diane's was a rambling story about two cats.

I have two cats, their names are Sam and Satine. They're very playful and fun. There's two sad things that happened to Sam. One thing is that part of his tail got cut off, and another thing is that his arm is broken. When we were on vacation, Sam and Satine crawled into a neighbor's car and fell asleep. When the man started driving, Satine crawled up the back of the seat and disturbed the man while he was driving. So the man took the cats and threw the cats out the window. Luckily another neighbor saw the cats and knew that Sam was ours, but the other cat he didn't know. So we got Sam back, but not Satine. So my mother started calling people, but no one saw Satine. Finally my brother found Satine.

On her next piece, Diane had received a lot of help. Consequently she'd focused on single incidents, recreating them in the present tense. She'd begun the piece with strong, active sentences:

> I was walking beside Jonathan's porch. All of a sudden I stepped in something. It made a "SCLAT" sound as it burst. We saw an army of bees charging at us. The noise was so loud that . . .

It was after this piece that Diane's despair set in. Day after day, Diane had begun a piece and then discarded it. Now we studied the abandoned pieces, trying to determine what had gone wrong. Had she been given too much help on her early pieces, and set too high a standard for herself? Did the trouble result from beginning every piece with a climactic moment, written in the present tense? Carolyn decided she'd ask Diane about it in the fall. "Maybe *she* can tell us what went wrong," she said.

Amy's writing seemed miraculous. While the factors which had influenced Susie's writing were usually clear, Amy's pieces seemed to emerge *ex nihilo*. She once described her writing process by saying, "When I write, it's like I have a movie in my mind and the words just come off of me. I'm like a typewriter, clicking off." Amy had strong creative powers, but she was less skillful at critiquing her own work. Consequently, her revisions were as likely to hurt as to help her writing, as in these two drafts of "What Should We Name Her?"

Draft 1

> I opened the door. "Hi" I said to my sister Linda. I walked by her. I stood stock still. I noticed something different. I walked back into the livingroom. No wonder what was different. She had a kitten! "Whose kitten is that?" I asked. I asked that because we don't have a kitten. "It's mine" she answered. The kitten was sitting in Linda's lap. The kitten looked like a fluffy puff ball. "What's the kitten's name?' I asked. "She doesn't have one". I wanted her name to be Pussywillow. Linda frowned and said it was a sissy's name. My mother came in. "I want to name her Fluffy." My mother was like the head of our house. I looked around at the faces staring at me, but they weren't staring at me, they were staring at my father. He came in and said in a deep, firm gruff voice, "The cat's name is Sidney". "I want it to be Fluffy", my mother said in a squeaky voice. "Then it will be her second name", my father said. "Sidney Fluffy," I said to myself. I though it was good. So that's why we named her Sidney.

Draft 2

"I want to name her Tiger" I said. Then my mother said in her high squeaky voice, "I want to name her Fluffy". We were all arguing about what we should name the kitten my sister had gotten in school. "How about Marshmellow", I suggested, "I still want Fluffy" my mother said again. Suddenly Linda said, "I want to name her Princess". "How about Queeny," my mother said in an anxious voice. "Mom that's a corny name" I said angrily. I glanced at the clock, it was five o'clock. My father would be home any minute. He walked through the door. He came into the room and said in his deep gruff voice, "The cat's name is Sidney". Everyone but my mother like the name. She sat around pouting. "I want to name her Fluff" she said. "Then that will be her second name", said my father. That seemed to fit her. That's how we named Sidney.

There were other children to talk about as well: Kenny, who shared some of Craig's problems; Trish, who was probably the best writer in the room; Jeremy, who wrote about granite quarries, explosions and space rather than about incidents from his life. And the list continued.

Only after we'd talked about the children did we consider the curriculum. Carolyn told us she would pattern her writing program after Pat's. The children would write four times a week, from 11:00 until 12:15. Each session would begin with a mini-lesson, then a workshop, and finally some form of sharing. But Carolyn was less sure of the details: room arrangements, writing folders, kinds of paper, methods of publishing, grades, and so forth. We started with the room.

In her notebook, Carolyn had listed the areas she wanted to include in her room. We went over the list together and Pat made more suggestions until the list read like this:

1. One corner with a rug for independent reading, share meetings and peer conferences.

2. Library area for literature and children's published books. Perhaps along the perimeter of the rug?

3. Editing area: round table with several chairs, red pens, editing guidesheets, dictionaries, etc.

4. Writing center: box of daily writing folders, color-coded for easy access; file drawer of cumulative writing folders; paper—yellow for rough drafts and white for final drafts; also scissors, tape, paste, white-out.
5. Bulletin board for displaying "Author of the Week," etc.
6. Places for peer conferences—on edges of the room.
Perhaps the floor is more practical than chairs. Carpet squares?

In her visits to room 209, Carolyn had seen children staple their final pieces onto rough drafts, filing the papers into cumulative writing folders. "But I didn't see any publishing," Carolyn said to Pat. "I must have overlooked it."

Pat shook her head. "I'm afraid you saw all there was to see," she said, then hurried to add, "Don't follow my example with publishing. Mary Ellen would be a better person to talk with about publishing." Mrs. Giacobbe's first graders had published 400 hardcover books that year. The blank books had been made by the children's parents at a wine and cheese party in September. Each book was covered with wallpaper, and the pages stitched together with dental floss. After children wrote three or four pieces, they selected their best, revised and edited them and then either Mrs. Giacobbe or a parent typed the pieces into a bound book. Midway through the year, call numbers and library cards had been added to the books and they were cataloged and grouped into a class library.

Carolyn knew of Mary Ellen Giacobbe's publishing efforts. She also knew of other teachers who typed children's writing onto ditto paper and distributed copies to the entire class. What was newer and stranger to her was hearing that Pat Howard's children had enthusiastically written and revised despite a lack of publishing.

Pat admitted that she, too, had been surprised. "I meant to publish their writing," she said, "but there wasn't time . . . and surprisingly, the kids didn't seem to miss it all that much." Once again she added, "Don't follow my example!" As we talked about it, Pat made an important observation. She said, "The crucial thing for my children was having readers—not just when the piece was done, but throughout the process. Sharing writing was essential: actually binding the stories into published books was less essential." And so our discussion of publishing turned into a discussion of sharing.

Pat Howard had found many ways to encourage sharing and now each method was added into the spiral notebook.
1. Share meetings. The whole class meets on the rug and

several children read, one at a time. After each child reads, he or she calls on friends for their responses or questions. The teacher encourages children to follow a line of questions.

2. Writers' Circle. Children are divided into clusters of three or four. The clusters meet simultaneously, with children within each cluster taking turns reading their writing aloud and receiving responses or questions from the others in their circle.

3. Quiet Share. For final moments of a class, each writer is asked to find readers who will read his or her piece and write responses on an attached index card.

4. Focused Share. The entire class meets together and shares with each other a specific aspect of their writing: their lead, their title, their main idea, their best descriptive passage.

5. Process Share. Children meet in one configuration or another to share their process rather than their products. Discussion centers on questions such as these:
   - What kinds of problems do you run into during writing? How do you go about solving them?
   - What changes did you make between first and final drafts? How did you go about making them? What prompted you to make the changes?
   - What are you planning to do next with your writing?

Each of these methods for sharing writing could also be described as a method for giving feedback on writing, and Carolyn noticed this. "Shouldn't there also be a time for celebrating rather than only for giving feedback—especially when it is finished writing?"

In his book, *Writing With Power*, Elbow makes the same point. He says,

> The essential human act at the heart of writing is the act of giving. There's something implacable and irreducible about it . . . it is a gift of yourself. . . . This central act of giving is curiously neglected in most writing instruction. . . . I'm embarrassed that it took me so long not just to understand the importance of sharing, but even to see it—to realize that there was something else useful you could do with a piece of writing besides giving feedback on it. . . . The reason it took me so long, I suspect, is that I am primarily an English teacher, and the reason I am beginning to notice sharing is that I am beginning to be a writer. Writers are more apt to understand writing as giving: "Here. Take it. Enjoy it. Thank me. . . . But I'm not interested right now in evaluation or criticism." (p. 21)

And so a sixth method of sharing was added to the spiral notebook:

6. Giving Writing. Children may read their piece aloud or give copies to friends, family or the class library—but the purpose is to give and to celebrate that giving.

Carolyn had another question. Most of Pat's children seemed to write only personal narratives. Was there a reason for not writing letters, fiction, poetry and reports?

Once again, Pat said, "Don't *follow* my example, improve on it." There had been good reasons, Pat felt, for launching the writing workshop by having children write about topics they knew and cared about—which had meant personal narratives and reports on children's projects, hobbies and areas of expertise. The children had invested themselves in their writing because they wrote on topics they cared about. Many of their first revisions resulted from seeing an incongruity between the subject matter which they knew so well, and the words they'd put onto the paper. Conferences were easy when children wrote personal narratives. Pat only needed to say, "Tell me what happened" and then, later, "Did you put all that down?"

The reasons for remaining in the personal narrative mode had not been good ones, but human ones. "I'm scared of poetry—hate it," Pat said, "and I've had bad teaching experiences with fiction. The kids just tell those space stories and copy television programs they've seen." But there was no denying that the children needed a chance to write in different modes—and that they'd need help in doing it.

The muffins were gone by then, and I was no longer feeling sad about my graduation from third grade into fourth. The remaining questions were put aside until September.

Pat and I left the house together. We stood for a moment between the two cars. Instead of saying goodbye, Pat said, "Jean Robbins just spoke to me. Next year I'm being moved to the fifth grade." She seemed strangely awkward, embarrassed.

I tried to reassure her that I thought fifth grade would be great—"Imagine the stories those older kids will write! " I said.

"I'll be teaching math."

"Just math?"

Pat nodded. "Each of the fifth grade teachers will have a specialty . . . and mine will be math." We walked toward her car. "You know, Lucy. I kept thinking this morning how it's all the same. I can teach math the way we've done writing: watching the kids, giving them time, turning class into a workshop . . ."

We hugged each other and I turned toward my red Subaru. "I wouldn't mind doing research in her math class," I thought. But there was Carolyn, waving at me from the house.

"See you in September," she called.

16. Twenty-six teachers in this classroom

September came, and I found that Mrs. Currier had indeed patterned her writing workshop after Mrs. Howard's. But there was a remarkably different aura in her classroom. While Mrs. Howard had been vivacious, quick to laugh and quick to anger, full of her own energy, ideas and momentum, Mrs. Currier had a gentler spirit. Once I watched her gather the children together and, with tears in her eyes, tell them, "Mrs. Currier has a spelling problem. *I* don't always get words right so you must help me." Often when the children came for help with their writing, Mrs. Currier would tell them, "I don't know what you can do to improve your story. You see, I'm just learning too." Her emphasis was on helping children to help each other. "There are twenty-six writing teachers in this classroom," she'd tell the children. "Each one of you has to be a writing teacher. You have to help each other because Mrs. Currier is not an expert on writing."

The children grew to respect the importance of being good helpers. In many classrooms, the best artist and the best math student are respected by their classmates. Similarly, visitors to Mrs. Currier's room were often told, "You should talk to that kid, he's a great conferencer." Although Susie was not considered the best writer in the room, the consensus seemed to be that she was the best writing teacher. Diane said it well. "Susie's the one I can barely say 'no' to. Her ideas for my writing are always good and she knows how not to hurt me."

But it was not only Susie who was skillful at peer conferences. All the children were better at helping each other than they had been in third grade. Conceivably this was because they were nine years old now and growing in their ability to view things through someone else's perspective. But I think more likely it was because the children sensed Mrs. Currier's goodness and responded in kind. They were good to her and good to each other. The year was not a thrilling one with each day bringing new and exciting adventures, but the children learned to trust and to help each other. In retrospect, I wonder if anything could have been more important for preadolescents and for writers.

Above all, Mrs. Currier was extremely careful to help children be good to each other. In a class share meeting, for example, if a youngster didn't seem to be listening, she'd quietly say to the writer, "Would you read your story over? I don't think we were all able to hear it." And if one child was hurtful to another—even in the roll of their eyes—Mrs. Currier would stop everything and talk about how writers need to trust their audience. She demonstrated a respect for other people, expected it from the children, and insisted on it. And so, at an age when children often grow increasingly self-conscious and hesitant to share, her children grew more trusting and more able to help each other.

Children who had problems with writing flourished in such an environment. Kelly, a little girl who had been crippled by cerebral palsy, learned to poke her way through typewritten stories. Kelly's stories were often just a few lines, but the class treated them with just as much respect as the long and elaborate stories written by Birger, Trisha, Diane, Amy, Brad, Susie and others. Because the class saw revision as a way to celebrate and build upon the potential of a piece, they usually revised their best work. At the end of Kelly's typewritten rough drafts, she would add new information resulting from a conference with a friend:

One night We when some where. Then We came back and we where looking for Samatha. WE couldn't find her. We looked everywhere. The babies where hugery so my father's girl friend and my sister want down to the store and got some caned milk and four eye drops. She took the caned milk and mixed it with warm water. Then she took one kitten and fed him with the eye drop full of midk and The She had fed all of the kittens a little be cause they all ready been fed some milk to them. I sarted crying because I thought the kittens where cold. Then my sister and I want to bed. Then my father went to look for Samatha and We found her, I was so happy when my father found her. because

I Thought Samatha got killed lots to visit some Friends gott a

THE END

Craig, too, flourished in this classroom. Not only his skills but also his self-concept grew stronger, and his gentle side became more evident. Instead of writing about angry topics, as he had done in the "Goofy" story and in many of his third-grade pieces, Craig began to write stories which were filled with tenderness, such as this beginning to his report about the white-tailed deer:

My Report on White Tail Deer

The baby fawn is awaken by a twig snap. He looks around it sees a bear coming toward him. He doesn't move, a flicker or even a eye. The bear sniffs the fawn. The bear leaves because it thinks the fawn is dead but really the fawn is alive and this is how the fawn fool the bear. After the enemy leaves, the fawn feels much more safe. About five minutes later the fawn hears an animal coming where the fawn is. The fawn sees the animal the animal is the fawns mother. Now the fawn knows it is safe for sure.

This report was not Craig's first draft. Like the others in his classroom, Craig sometimes wrote five or six drafts of a piece. Usually he wrote at least three drafts, often without conferences with Mrs. Currier. Because the children were good at helping each other, Mrs. Currier's youngsters were able to carry on about their work in an independent fashion. The classroom felt like an artist's studio, with youngsters at work in their craft. When visitors stopped by, they'd usually find several children rehearsing for writing while others were immersed in drafts. A few students might have red pen in hand, a sure sign that they were editing. One or two children might be at the back of the classroom, reading homemade books filled with final drafts. Others would be writing to a pen pal. Often two or three children were just drifting about, disconnected from their work. Invariably, six or eight youngsters would be conferring with each other. Sometimes it would take a few minutes before the visitor saw Carolyn, for she would be moving quietly about the room helping children to help each other.

17. Peer conferences thread through the writing process

When I work with teachers who are trying to follow "the Atkinson model," I find they are often unaware that at Atkinson, peer conferences occurred throughout the entire writing process. Conferences weren't postponed until a child had completed a draft; instead, these interactions were interwoven throughout the evolution of a piece, sustaining and extending its life-force. In this chapter, I will try to show some of the different kinds of conferences which occurred in the classroom during the writing process.

It was not unusual for the children to help each other with topic selection. During the fall of fourth grade, I watched Diane sit restlessly over a paper entitled "Topic Ideas." Fifteen minutes went by, and still the paper was blank. I wondered if Diane's third grade problems with writing had spilled into fourth grade. But then Diane pulled a chair alongside her best friend's desk. "I keep giving up on my stories," she said. "I go to put them in my folder and there are four others there I still have to finish. Now I'm out of ideas."

"How about the summer?" Susie asked. "What did you do?"

"Just swam."

"Was there any time when swimming was interesting?"

"I just swam with Debbie."

"Any fun times you had?" Susie asked, still hopeful.

"Well, I played seesaw with a friend, and I went canoeing."

Susie's face lit up. "Why don't you write about canoeing?" she said, encouraging Diane.

"I was embarrassed. The neighbor made me sing fairy-tale songs," Diane answered, but this time there was new energy in her voice. "I guess I *do* have some ideas." And Diane returned to her desk to jot down this list:

Choppy Waters
A Wet Surprise
393 Steps to Go
Puppet Show

Within a few minutes, Diane had a beginning and, interestingly, it was to an entirely different topic.

> Amy and I hopped onto the sailboat, pulling her uncle in.
> "Ready?" he asked.
> "Okay," we both said. The wind blew wildly as we took off.

Susie had helped Diane brainstorm for topics, but Diane had steered clear of Susie's choice of topics. These girls and their friends prided themselves on independence, and as part of this, on choosing their own topics. For this reason they were disdainful of the "Voting Box," a topic-selection system invented by Birger and used by many of the boys. The boys selected their topics by brainstorming a list of possibilities and then taking their lists from classmate to classmate, gathering votes.

Topics	Votes
- Norway	X X X
- I liked the playground the way it was!	X X
- We were going to a movie.	X X X
- The lady sat next to us.	X X X X X

Once when Birger came to Susie with his tally sheet, and asked her to vote for her favorite topic from his list, Susie took it to her friends and, with much giggling, they added scores of checks alongside each topic, thereby thwarting his system and forcing Birger to make his own decision. I enjoyed the scene heartily, for although I didn't confess it, I'd never been very fond of the voting box. The real coup, however, came a few weeks later. Birger had listed possible topics and carefully drawn his voting box. Then, alone at his desk, he started adding votes to his box. "One vote for number two," he said, "and one vote for number four." Like the announcer at the racetrack, he continued, "Two votes for number three, one for number one . . . " until finally he announced, "And the winner is: number three!"

Just when Birger and many of the boys became more independent in their topic selection, there was a flurry of interest among Susie and her friends for stories which starred and co-starred each other. Susie wrote several consecutive stories about adventures she'd shared with Diane. Diane returned the favor, until Amy slept over at Diane's house. That week Diane gave up on a story about Susie and started a new piece, "Playing with Amy on the Garage Roof." At this point, Susie returned to stories about her mother and her dog Caspar. During those months, it seemed that the rise and fall of friendships could be plotted in the topics children chose. When I asked Susie about this, she indicated that the point was not so much to write pieces which honored a friendship, but to have companionship during writing time. She explained, "I write about my friends if I'm on good terms with them. Then I'll go over and say, 'Remember when we did this and that?' and I get all excited and build it up." She added, "It helps me when people push me on like that. I keep going more if people want my story."

After deciding on a topic, these young writers sometimes worked on their own for several days, reemerging with a draft in hand. Just as often, their interactions with each other continued. When Diane was caught in a writer's block—not an uncommon thing for her—she often relied on Susie to prompt her beyond the stalemate. "I don't know why, but it helps her to say the story out loud," Susie explained. And so when Diane told Susie she only knew boring stuff about beavers and therefore couldn't find a good beginning for her report, Susie, quite predictably, asked Diane questions about beavers. "Why did you decide to write about them?" "Imagine you were a beaver, how would you work?" "How would you feel?" Her questions yielded results. "I'd feel wet!" Diane answered, laughing, "and muddy. They carry mud on their tails, their strong tails scoop up mud and then splash it on the dam."

"Hey Di, that sounds good!" Susie said, paraphrasing Diane's description of how beavers work.

Nothing could stop Diane now. She started talking quickly, no longer needing Susie to prompt her with questions. "On the side of the river there is soft mud. And they start digging and digging and sometimes water starts splurting in and their lodge over-flows."

Susie, meanwhile, was leaning forward at her desk, following Diane's every word. It was as if, at that moment, nothing in the world was more interesting to Susie than beavers. "Once I saw a thing about beavers and it was sad because a family of beavers froze," she said, adding on to Diane's information. "We have warm houses and they don't."

Diane nodded. "The growing of beavers is sad, too. The babies get kicked out when they begin to grow up and it's crowded. I don't think that's fair. The adults should get kicked out." Then Diane looked about the room, making sure no one was listening. She lowered her voice. "The mating seasons are yucky. Boy and girl beavers go into the lodge. I can't say what happens." She paused, significantly, then continued in a stage whisper. "They mate, and the female lays down and the male stands up. But beavers don't usually stand up because their head hits the top of the lodge. And the water starts to come in and the female has to move. But she's kind of heavy (if you know what I mean)." The girls giggled at this reference to the weight of pregnancy.

Susie redirected Diane's attention to the empty page. "Before you started to talk, you weren't much interested, and now you are talking and talking," she said.

"But if I put all this down, it'll be five pages!"

"Is that bad?"

But Susie's question was unnecessary, for Diane had already begun to write.

On that particular morning, Diane did not experiment with different leads, but on many other occasions she did, and sometimes she involved Susie in that phase of her writing. Once when both Diane and Susie were writing about a puppet show they'd produced together, Diane asked Susie, "How should I start it? Should I say, 'Susie,' I yelled?"

Susie's answer couldn't have been more appropriate. "Try it," she said. "Try it; why not?"

Susie not only gave help on leads, she also received it. As we saw earlier, her classmates helped simply by listening, providing an external executive function for Susie. When she was able to talk about a lead, it was far more likely that her next lead would take a different tack on the subject rather than simply continuing with the same sequence of events.

Sometimes Susie also benefited from talking with her friends about the qualities of a good lead. Once when she and Birger were reading through the wallpaper books which held their final drafts, Birger called Susie's attention to the way he started his pieces. "They're all the same!" he noticed. "My leads are all sound effects." Then he turned the pages of his book, reading off each lead:

- Zoom. I rode right past my grandfather.
- Puff, puff. I ran exhaustedly down the road.
- "I know my way through here easy," I said, unsurely.
- "Arrr!" I put my brake on. I was going over to Trevor's.

Susie was excited and Birger dismayed by their discovery. "If I was a professional," Birger said, "they'd probably give up on reading my books 'cause they'd all be the same."

Once they had chosen and written leads, children might spend as much as several hours, or as little as several minutes, on a draft. When I tell this to teachers, they often comment, "But my children's attention spans could never last an hour!" Neither did these children's. Instead, the youngsters moved in and out of an immersion in their work. Sometimes they'd grasp their pencils tightly, lean low over their papers, and block out the rest of the world. Other times, they'd lean back in their chairs, surveying their work, scanning the classroom.

In Mrs. Giocobbe's first grade, children usually carried on a running monologue during these interludes. "Okay, now I've done four pages," a child might say, "and I drawed a pretty dress, and now I have three more pages to go, and what will I tell, let's see . . ."

In fourth grade, children were more apt to use these interludes as a time for brief discussions with each other. Often, like artists in a studio, they just shared thoughts about their craft. Diane looked up from her first draft and said, to no one in particular, "I can tell I'll have lots of drafts. It's because I like the story. If I don't like it, I just fix it up on the same paper."

Susie, who hadn't seemed to be listening at all, responded without looking up from her paper. "Same here. I work harder when I like the story." Then she continued with her writing, and Diane tried another friend.

"Hey, Wendy, you know, I'm going to have the same luck as you. You know how you used to do mounds and mounds of drafts. Now I'm going to have to do that, too!" Wendy didn't respond; she too was involved in her work. So Diane reread her story and soon she too was writing.

Although neither Mrs. Howard nor Mrs. Currier commented on the correctness of a child's draft until the writer had revised the piece for content and was ready to edit, it was not unusual for children to chat about their spelling or punctuation during the process of drafting a piece.

"If you want to add excitement to your stories, put in these 'explanation marks'," a child told his friend.

"I don't know whether to say the bear was 'big'—or 'enormous'," Susie mused, then solved the quandary by choosing 'big,' then adding three exclamation marks.

Diane once turned to Amy and said, "I know this is a weird question, but I haven't used this word in a long time. How do you spell *very*?" Another time she asked Susie, "If you ran to a bench and lay down, what do you write? *Laid* down?"

Although these informal conferences punctuated the entire writing process, more formal and extended conferences occurred when drafts were completed. These conferences took on many different forms and served many different purposes. Often, for these conferences, children would leave their desks and go either to a conference table at the back of the room or to the rug in their reading area. Almost always, listeners would listen to the story and then respond to the content. When Diane heard Susie's tale, "Getting My Ears Pierced," Diane's first response was to exclaim, "I hope that sign 'Ears Pierced' is still at the mall when I go!"

When Trevor heard Birger's story, "A Shadow at the Fire," he too responded to the content. "When you said you ran into the house because you thought somebody was going to come and get you, I've had that feeling before. In the middle of the night, if your dog just turns over, you can get it."

Sometimes the listeners weren't quite able to understand their friend's text, and their perplexed questions usually led the writer toward revision, as in this interchange between Diane and Susie:

Diane: Your story is called "The Swinging Vines" but what were the swinging vines? Did you go in little carts?
Susie: You mean you can't picture it?
Diane: No.
Susie: Oh, then I'll describe it more. (She writes herself a note to do this in the next draft.)

Oftentimes listeners diagnosed a problem in the story, and deliberately asked questions aimed at helping the writer repair that problem. After I listened to a conference between Birger and Gina, I asked them to tell me what questions were most helpful in a conference. Birger answered, "Like if it's a boring story about a tree fort, you could ask, 'What happened up there that was exciting? Did you ever get stuck up there?' " Gina agreed, adding, "And sometimes they need to describe it more, so I get them to tell me how things looked, then I ask if they could fit that into their story." The following transcripts record several conferences in which children seemed to ask leading questions. You will notice, however, that the control of the conference never entirely leaves the writer's hands:

Susie read to Diane and Amy a draft about a chickadee which came and stood on her outstretched hand, pecking at some seed which she held out for him.

Amy: Good! What happens next?
Susie: He looks at me, then quickly hops on my hand.
Diane: How did it feel?
Susie: It tickled . . . not like needles, just a nice, little hold.
Diane: I've had that feeling before.
Susie: I didn't realize, but I should add that in.
Diane: I think it adds a lot to your story to tell that.
Amy: Do you need any other help?
Susie: Do you like the lead, or do you think I should start it when the chickadee lands on my hand?

Amy: I like it the way you have it. What were you thinking when you were standing there and the bird didn't come to you?

Susie: I was thinking it was too bad they don't understand about how I wasn't going to hurt them. I might add that, too. Thanks.

Susie reads the story about meeting her grandparents in the Florida airport.

Diane: Do you like your story?

Susie: I don't know yet. I gotta go and see . . .

Diane: and . . .

Susie: And I need help at the end of it.

Diane: (asking about the section which came at the end) How did you feel about seeing your grandparents?

Susie: I felt like running, but I don't know if I did. They looked so different and I was so glad to see them. Should I add that?

Diane: Yeah, maybe.

As I studied transcripts from the peer conferences, it seemed that Susie, more than most children, tended to tell writers about the problems she saw in their drafts. Instead of asking leading questions to solve the dilemma, she just raised the issue, leaving the writer to solve it later on. When Tricia wrote a first-person narrative about herself as a four-year-old, Susie reminded her that her main character would have to think like a four-year-old. "Remember," she warned, "they don't have as much worries as we older people do." Similarly, in a conference with Birger, Susie tried to explain to him the problem she saw in his draft. Birger began the conference by reading his draft:

"Come on, it's our turn for the raft," my cousin yelled. I was in Norway, and we'd just gotten off the raft, Joanne and Cecilie and me. Joanne is tall, has a good imaginative mind. She has short blonde hair and has a high temper . . .

Susie: I like it, but you tell about the raft and then stop and describe the people and then go back to the raft again. It's like you take one part and divide it up with description. But I *do* like how you describe people. Maybe you could . . .

Birger: (interrupting her) . . . put the description at the beginning?

Susie: Or tell it as part of the story. Like, Birger, if the fat lady was going up the stairs, describe how she was fat by showing how she goes up the stairs.

Birger: Yeah, so I could describe them at the same time I tell about the raft. (He looks at his paper.)

Susie: Oh, Birger, could I say one thing? You describe them, like you said, 'she had an imaginative mind,' but could you describe it in a way that has to do with the story?

Birger returned to his desk, thanking Susie for her assistance. Susie nodded, unaware that she had not only given but received help. For although we billed these interactions as *writing* conferences, they were, in reality, *language* conferences. Children used and developed skills in reading, listening and speaking as well as in writing. And although we assumed that their purpose was to help the writer, in reality, the learning was collaborative and mutual. Both the writer and the listener helped each other.

18. Teaching children to teach each other

"Not my children," teachers often say when they hear about Atkinson. "If I let my kids get together and talk about their writing, they'd write each other's pieces; either that or they'd tell each other their stories are perfect." Others feel even more strongly. "I tell my students there's no talking during writing time. Otherwise it's chaos."

Carolyn was skillful at responding to these comments because she'd heard them from many of the visitors who streamed through her classroom that year. "I felt the same way," she'd reassure them. "But then I realized I was expecting my kids to confer well without giving them any help. I don't expect them to learn math without guidance. Why should I expect conferencing to be a natural skill?"

Often during that year, Mrs. Currier used mini-lessons as a time to teach the skills of peer conferencing. She had begun this with my urging. With much trepidation, Mrs. Currier and Diane held a public conference in front of the classroom. First, Diane read her draft and her teacher responded to it, receiving the piece, asking questions, and helping Diane reconsider what she'd done. Then roles were switched, and Mrs. Currier read a story she'd written for the occasion and Diane listened and responded to it. After the demonstration, Mrs. Currier asked the class to replay the conferences, thinking about what worked and what didn't work. Soon these public conferences became commonplace. Mrs. Currier used them to illustrate ways the children could become good listeners, and to warn children against taking control away from the writer. Mostly, she used them to show the importance of asking good conference questions.

On one wintry morning, Mrs. Currier began the mini-lesson by asking children to list ten questions they wished others would ask them in conference. Then they shared the questions, discussed them, and eventually compiled a huge chart entitled "Good Conference Questions." These were the questions Susie hoped others would ask her:

1. How do you like your story? How do you feel about it?
2. Does your title fit your story?
3. Do you have more than one story in your piece?
4. Can you add more feeling to it?
5. Is there more you could add?
6. Tell me what happened in detail.
7. Are there too many extra things in it that you don't really need?
8. Are you going to keep working on it?
9. Have you enjoyed writing it?

Share meetings, like mini-lessons, were a vehicle for helping children become good writing teachers. When children shared work-in-progress at these whole-class meetings, Mrs. Currier suggested that both the writer and the listener follow a format which they could also use in all peer conferences:

1. Writers would begin by explaining where they were in the writing process, and what help they needed. For example, a child might say, "I'm on my third draft and I want to know if you can picture it," or "I have six titles and I can't decide which is best."
2. Usually, but not always, the writer then would read the piece—or the pertinent section of the piece—out loud.
3. The writer would call on listeners. Usually listeners would begin by retelling what they'd heard, "I learned that . . . " they'd say, or "Your piece began . . . " Sometimes they'd begin by responding to or appreciating the content of the piece.
4. Questions or suggestions would then be offered, not about everything, but about the concern raised by the writer. Sometimes other things would come up as well, but not always.

Mrs. Currier, like Mrs. Howard, used share meetings as a time when she could teach children to follow a line of questioning. This is a crucial skill in conferencing and a difficult one. Oftentimes, whether children were in a group or in an individual peer conference, they were apt to hop from one topic to another, as they do in this very typical interaction:

Listener #1: Where are you in this story?
    Writer: I was sitting on the boat.
Listener #2: What happens next in the story? How does it end?
At this point in the discussion, Mrs. Currier intervened, reminding children to follow through on one question before moving on to the next. The discussion then backtracked and continued like this:

Listener #1: Where were you in this story?
Writer: I was sitting on the boat.
Listener #2: Exactly where were you?
Writer: Well, I sat up in the bow of the boat with my legs hanging over the edge. I was looking out to sea.
Listener #1: Now I can picture it! Do you think you should add that in, because it was confusing to not know where you were in the story.
Writer: I'll look at it and see if it goes in. Any other questions or suggestions?

As the children learned to follow through on questions, the share meetings became more helpful for them as writers. Instead of a barrage of connected ideas and questions, writers and listeners worked together to develop a train of thought and to explore the ramifications of their ideas. In February, Jay read a draft aloud to his classmates. It was a detailed story of one of his earlier escapades. Jay had crept past a lady and into a chicken coop, stolen eggs from behind the curtains and then hidden the eggs.

The children clapped when Jay finished his story. It was rare for them to clap during their share meeting, and so Jay seemed delighted with their celebration of his story. Jay blushed and almost forgot to call on classmates for their questions and comments.

Craig: Jay, why did you hide the eggs? I don't get that part.
Jay: So no one would find them. I shouldn't have stolen them.
Susie: Who is the lady?
Jay: Just a lady.
Diane: Is she important in the story? Do we need to know . . .
Craig: (interrupting) You could tell about her hair and her eyes and her clothes and all.
Jay: But it isn't important. That's not part of the story. (He seemed frustrated.)
Mrs. Currier: Jay, you've mentioned someone in the story, this lady, and so we need to know just a little. Maybe a word or two would be enough.
Jay: Well, I don't know what to say. I can't remember. She was just sitting there and they were her chickens.
Mrs. Currier: Oh, I see. So you put her into the story because they were *her* chickens!

> Jay: Oh, I could tell that . . .
>
> Susie: Another thing, Jay. I didn't understand about the curtains. Why were the eggs behind the curtains? What curtains?
>
> Jay: They were at the nests so the chickens could lay their eggs in peace.
>
> Susie: Oh! Well, I really liked your story, Jay, because, except for that one part, I could picture all of it and how it felt. I never thought you would have taken eggs when you were little!

The children became more skillful at helping each other as they learned more about the qualities of good writing. Mostly they learned this through writing and rewriting, but to some degree, the mini-lessons on specific points also contributed. Usually Mrs. Currier used the share meetings as a time to reinforce the concepts raised in mini-lessons. For example, on a morning in late February Mrs. Currier devoted the mini-lesson to the concept of "show—not tell." When Wendy came to her during the workshop for more help with the concept, Mrs. Currier suggested Wendy save her questions until the share meeting. When all the children had gathered on the rug, Wendy explained her predicament. "I'm trying to show that I was riding along on a snowmobile without *saying*, 'I rode on a snowmobile.' This is what I have so far:"

> My father and I were riding in the snowmobile. We went over the ice and through some woods and up to the Kingston fire tower but all I could see when I look around was trees and woods.
>
> We zoomed on and got onto ice that had no snow on top of it. My father tried to steer and all of a sudden . . . we were fishtailing!

Amy raised her hand. "You could say, 'The snow was spraying in my face or the trees raced by'—give them a feeling of it being fast."

Susie added, "And instead of saying 'we were on a snowmobile,' Wendy, you could say, 'I climbed onto our big yellow snowmobile. My father climbed on beside me. He said 'hold on' and we zoomed off.'"

Similarly, on a day when Mrs. Currier had devoted the mini-lesson to the effective use of dialogue and to the problems of overusing it, she suggested that Tracey bring her draft to the share meeting. Tracey explained to her friends, "I can't seem to get all the chitchat out of my story," and then she read her draft to the class. This is the beginning of it:

> Billie and I went on a snowbank. Billie Jean buried herself. I said, "What in the world are you doing?"

"Burying myself."

"Oh. Get out from under there you Stupid. You look just like a snowman."

"Well, if I do? Poo! Poo!"

"Oh shut up." My sister buried herself again. "Well if you buried yourself, I will too."

Wendy began with a question which was neither tactful nor related to the issue at hand. "Was there anything else you did outside that would make a more interesting story?" she asked.

Mrs. Currier quietly interrupted. "Wendy, do you remember the specific thing Tracey wanted us to help her with?"

Wendy looked down and began picking at her sneaker. Susie came to her rescue with a suggestion for Tracey. "In some places where you or Billie Jean are talking, could you make yourselves *thinking* instead of talking? Like, you could say 'In my mind I thought she looked like a snowman.'"

There were other questions and suggestions and more of them reinforced the morning's mini-lesson on dialogue. The children's questions during share meetings did something else as well. They provided models for good questions, and for questions which developed specific qualities of good writing. Although the class never gathered these questions into a chart, they easily could have compiled something like this:

Questions which help writers focus:
- What is the most important thing you are saying?
- Why did you choose this topic? What's important about it to you?
- Which is the most important part of your story? Why?
- Where do you get to your main idea?
- Is there anything that doesn't seem to fit into your story?
- Do you think you have two stories, or one?

Questions which help writers "show—not tell:"
- Read me the places where you're pleased with your description. What makes these sections work better than others?
- Are there places you could describe more? I can't always picture it.
- Have you tried to underline the places where you *tell* us something like "he was ugly," and then rewrite those on another sheet of paper, showing instead of telling?
- If I'd been watching you, how would I have known that—as you say in the paper—you felt sad? What exactly would I have seen?

Questions which help writers expand their pieces:
- In your own words, tell me all about this. What else do you know about the topic?

- What questions do you think people will have for you? If you answer them now, you can get rid of some of the questions.
- Could you go through your story, reading me a line, then telling me more about it?
- Why don't you try reading your story over and putting a dot on the page wherever there is more to tell.

Questions which help a writer reconsider the sequence:

- Let's see; what did you tell first? Second? Third? (They make a list.) Is there any other way you could order this? Why did you decide to put it in this order?
- Have you tried cutting it up and putting it in a different order?
- Could you make this into a flashback?

Although both mini-lessons and share meetings were helpful, I suspect they weren't nearly as powerful as the example Mrs. Currier set in her own conferences with the children.

19. Teaching by example

As I look back over the data from the NIE study, I see patterns emerge. In some of the classrooms, teacher:child conferences became models for child:child conferences. In these classrooms, teachers interacted with children in such a way that children learned how to interact with each other. Children began asking each other the questions which had been asked of them.

This happened in Mary Ellen Giacobbe's first grade and in Carolyn Currier's fourth grade. But it happened less in Pat Howard's classroom and even less in some others. Why? Our data suggest, and I believe, that teacher:child conferences provide a model for peer conferences when they are structured in ways which help children assume responsibility and ownership of their craft.

We never talked about this during the study, but I think some teachers felt their job in a conference was to teach the writer, while others felt it was to teach the writing. In order to improve a child's text, some teachers rushed into a conference with evaluations, suggestions and directions. With the best of intentions, they'd say to a child, "The beginning needs work, doesn't it. Why don't you see if there's another sentence later on in this paragraph which might make a better lead." These teachers probably never considered that the lasting effect of such a conference was that children were kept on writer's welfare. As teachers, we've all done our share of perpetuating children's dependence on our ideas. I, too, have approached a conference thinking, "What would I do if this draft were mine? How would I improve on it?" Somehow it's so much easier to write someone else's piece than to write my own! Sometimes I've quite literally taken the writing out of a writer's hands and held it in my own: what a message. Taking control has also come in the form of my speaking first. I assume the writer has nothing to say, that he or she is a blank slate waiting for my wisdom, and so I impose my agenda onto the conference. Specific questions, meant to coax writers to expand my favorite sections, are another way of taking over a child's draft. "What color were the flowers?" I ask, implying that this information belongs in the draft. But who is to say if the color of the flowers was important to the writer?

Donaldson speaks eloquently about the issue of control:

> Exercise such control as is needful with a light touch and never relish the need . . . [for] a great deal will depend on what the teacher sees the aim of control to be. . . . If the teacher obviously wants the children to become competent, self-determining, responsible beings and believes them capable of it, [then] the ultimate aim of control is to render itself unnecessary. (1978, p.126)

For Mrs. Currier, a light touch was second nature. Only with great hesitation would she suggest ways a child might improve a piece; she was far more apt to ask writers to tell her their plans or their difficulties. And so she often began a conference simply by asking, "How's it coming?" The writers would lead the way, teaching her about their work-in-progress and about their hopes and their problems with the writing. Just as a patient teaches the physician so that wise and pertinent help can be given, so too Mrs. Currier's children led the way in their conferences with her. "I don't think this part fits with the rest," one child would tell her. "I like it, it's my very very best," another child would announce. The children played an active role in their conferences with Mrs. Currier, and they held the dynamics of the conferences in their own hands. Their teacher wanted them to become competent, self-determining, responsible writers and critics, and she helped it to happen.

Our data from the NIE study also suggest that it was when teacher:child conferences were predictable that children were most likely to internalize the temporary structure—the scaffolding—of a conference. In classrooms where teachers' responses were ever-changing, kaleidoscope ones, children could not anticipate their teacher's responses. They used their time "reading" the teacher, rather than participating in the writing process.

I don't think it was intentional when Mrs. Giacobbe and Mrs. Currier built patterns into their conferences, but it was nevertheless effective. In most of her conferences, Mrs. Currier attended largely to the child's emerging subject; therefore, I call these content conferences. "Children need to know they are being heard," Mrs. Currier said, and this was her purpose in a content conference: to listen to the child's subject.

It's funny. I once thought listening was easy, that you just sit back and listen. Now I find that listening is the hardest thing to do. I once thought watching the ball in tennis was easy too. When I was a kid, my mother used to shout from across the net saying, "Keep your eye on the ball." I remember thinking, obviously you watch the ball. Obviously you listen.

But the other day on the tennis courts, I watched the ball—and it was an entirely new sensation. I was mesmerized by the ball;

watching it coming, as if in slow motion, then the bounce, the climb; then it hung, suspended for an instant. Why was that day different? Because I wasn't apologizing for my bad shots or tidying my hair. I wasn't thinking about myself.

Listening. For Mrs. Currier, this was the crux of all conferences, but especially the content conferences. The pattern in most content conferences was for Mrs. Currier to listen to the child's content and then to repeat the child's story, verifying that the meaning had been received. She might say, "Amy, you've really given me an image of that fox, lying in his den. I can just picture . . . " Or she might say, "Another exciting story, Birger! Whew. You're going to wear me out with all this excitement. Let's see, first you . . . " Sometimes this active listening involved questions which would clear away the snags and tangles preventing Mrs. Currier from receiving the child's message, but the focus was on what the child wanted to convey, not on trumped up questions meant to tug out more information. Ironically, such listening brings out more information than any amount of tugging and pulling. Listening helps writers believe in what they have to say.

Sometimes in her content conferences, Mrs. Currier helped writers to focus their subject or expand their information. Either way, she began the conference with listening and with letting the children know she'd heard them.

Whether the writer is a first grader whose story is a list, a fifth grader who tells about a whole summer without highlighting a specific theme, or a professional writer searching for the thread of his or her book, *focus* is a crucial concern. Mrs. Currier asked her children over and over, "What are you really saying here?" "What's the most important point?" "Why did you choose this topic—what is it that matters to you?" "What do you want to leave your reader with?" When I sent an early draft of this book to Frank Smith, he wrote in his review, "Calkins has three stories here. Does she want her focus to be on Susie, or on the teachers, or on what she learned as a researcher?" For us all, focus is a crucial concern.

Sometimes, Mrs. Currier's content conferences had a different purpose. If the piece was a skeleton, lacking details, or if the child had just focused a topic, Mrs. Currier's questions helped children *expand* their information. When Birger decided to cut in half his story about exchanging bottles for $2.50, focusing only on his bike accident on the way to the store, he worried that his piece would be awfully short. Mrs. Currier asked questions to help the boy realize how much he had to say. She did this with open-ended questions meant to tap Birger's energy. "What exactly happened, Birger?" "How did you feel?" "It is hard for me to imagine what it was like. Will you help me?"

Her children sometimes tested her interest. They'd give cursory answers, quick summaries. When this happens, it is easy to resort to milking the child for more information. It's easy to resort to asking specific questions, questions which tug more details from the writer. "How fast were you going?" "Did you think you would fall?" Sometimes these questions work, but more often, they only distract writers from what they have to say. So Mrs. Currier developed a more effective tactic. If children gave only sketchy, quick answers to her open-ended questions, she'd circle back to their story, asking them, "Will you tell me what happened again. Tell me the details so I can picture the whole thing." And then, to launch the story, she'd add, "How did it start?"

Sometimes she and the other teachers would phrase these questions differently, asking, for example:

So if I'd been standing there, what would I have seen?

or

If you were going to make a movie of that incident, what would I see happening first on that screen? How would it begin?

or

So, let me see if I got this right. It all started . . . how?

The significant thing about her questions—whether in the focus or the expanding conferences—was that Mrs. Currier left control in the writer's hands. She didn't pull children this way and that, distracting them from what they wanted to say. Also, the questions were usually universal questions. They could be asked of almost any piece of writing. It was not long before children were asking these same questions of each other.

What's the main thing you're trying to say?

Which is your favorite thing in your story?

Tell me in your own words exactly what happened.

Do you think that stuff you're telling me is important, that you should add it in . . . 'cause I do.

But then I noticed another kind of conference, and it seemed to come from nowhere. In their peer conferences, children began to ask each other about their process rather than just their subjects.

How may drafts did you do? How's this last draft different than the first one?

When you wrote this, did you get into any problems or did you just write it straight through?

What are you planning to do next?

Children not only asked each other process questions, they were also extraordinarily articulate when they answered those questions. They were very skillful at describing their own strategies for writing, at critically reviewing their methods, and at consciously guiding their thinking. This is what these fourth graders had to say about their writing.

Craig: If you are stuck on the beginning, you can write leads to get a good beginning. Leads can be for finding a subject or for getting a good start. But when I get a good lead I just keep it. It's a good lead if I get right into the story. I try to make the whole story interesting so the person reading it won't quit. When I can tell it is going to get boring, I make the ending.

Diane: Usually I try to get all I can out of a draft. I don't do the whole piece over just to add a word or two. So I have some drafts you can barely read, I've added so much, and crossed things out. I just keep going on the one draft until I can't get anything more in.

Birger: I've just made a discovery. I usually put people into my stories now because when there are other people than me in the story, then I don't have to say "I did this and I did that." Instead I can put the other people saying to each other, "Where did he go?" . . . I can have the other people do the talking, keeping things explained.

The children's ability to ask each other process questions and to describe their writing strategies had not emerged from nowhere. In this instance, I had been the model. Children were still asking each other the questions which had been asked of them—this time, not by their teacher so much as by their researcher. Day by day for two years, I'd asked these children: "What are you planning to do next?" "What new problems did you run into?" "How's this draft different than the earlier one?"

Because my questions, like Mrs. Currier's, had been predictable and universal questions, they were a powerful teaching force. I hadn't intended to teach the children but instead to understand them, yet I'd not only observed their growth, I'd also participated in it.

It was not only the children who began asking process questions, but their teacher as well. By the end of that year, Mrs. Currier was as apt to focus on a child's writing strategies as on his content. Both Carolyn and I are now convinced that these process conferences were as powerful as the content conferences. Because the children were reflecting on their strategies for writing, they were learning to direct their thinking. Donaldson, Vygotsky, Piaget, Cazden, Bruner and others have emphasized that aware-ness of one's own thinking marks a crucial step toward directing it. Bruner writes: "I suspect that much of growth starts out by turning around on our own traces and recording in new forms what we have been doing or seeing . . . We say, 'I see what I was doing now,' or 'So that's what the thing is'" (1966, p. 21).

Similarly, Vygotsky says, "control of a function is the counter-part of one's consciousness of it." He goes on to claim that the growth of "consciousness and deliberate mastery" are "the prin-cipal contributions of the school years" (1962, p. 90). Donaldson builds on Vygotsky's claim. She writes, "the point to grasp is how closely the growth of consciousness is related to the growth of the intellect. . . . If the intellectual powers are to develop, the child must gain a measure of control over his own thinking and he cannot control it while he remains unaware of it" (1978, p. 129).

When Mrs. Currier began talking with children about how they went about writing as well as what they wrote about, it led her to new ways of challenging the children. Sometimes she'd ask youngsters, "What are you planning to do next?" If children had no plans, Mrs. Currier might suggest they experiment with some strategies writers often use. For example, earlier we saw Mrs. Currier encouraging Susie to expand her two-page story into six pages. And, to some children, she might recommend that they break their story into parts and work on each part separately as if it were a whole story. Once she told the children about how writers sometimes cut their stories into parts and rearrange the sequence of the parts. "I want the kids to have a sense of their options, because I never knew about them when I was a child," she said. Sometimes, but rarely, this meant encouraging children to try something they never would have thought of on their own.

Originally the strategies came from Mrs. Currier and from knowledge she had gleaned from me and from books on what writers do with their drafts. But soon children were inventing and sharing their own strategies, and Mrs. Currier had only to direct them to use each other as resources, saying, "You might want to try what Susie did yesterday; do you remember how we talked about it at the end of the day?" or "Why don't you take this draft over to Craig and see if the two of you can come up with some good revision strategies you could experiment with."

A third kind of conference emerged in the classroom that year, and once again, my research had an input into these conferences. In order to document the children's developing ability to assess their own work critically and their emerging criteria for judging writing, I asked children questions such as these at regular intervals:

What do you have to do to be a good writer?

If you had a pile of stories, and you were going to divide them into two piles—good stories and bad stories—how would they be different?

Which is the best story you've written so far this year? Which is the next best? What makes one better than the next?

What makes for a good lead?

Initially, Mrs. Currier and I viewed these questions, like the process interviews, as part of research rather than teaching. But we soon found that because we asked children to look back and assess their work, the youngsters began to ask the same things of each other. In Mrs. Giacobbe's first grade, I watched Audrey read her story to a group of friends.

"It's good," six-year-old Chris said when Audrey was finished. "I like it."

Greg interrupted. "Chris, tell her on every page *what* you liked and then ask her for her favorite page."

Children also learned to evaluate their own emerging texts. A child would finish a draft and immediately her eyes would climb back up the page; the youngster would shift from being a writer to being a reader, reminding me of a quote by Ciardi: "The last act . . . of writing must be to become one's own reader. It is, I suppose, a schizophrenic process. To begin passionately and to end critically, to begin hot and to end cold; and, more important, to try to be passion-hot and critic-cold at the same time."

Because there was a predictable structure to our conferences with the children, because we asked predictable and universal questions and gave the children a sense of ownership and involvement, they began to internalize the conferences. Both the teacher:child conferences and the researcher:child conferences became models for the conferences children had with each other.

20. When children conference with themselves

"**Y**ou can conference with yourself," Diane told me in fourth grade. She went on to explain, "You just read the piece over to yourself and it's like there is another person there and you think thoughts to yourself of what is wrong with it." By writing for readers, Diane had learned to write with a reader perched on her shoulder. She continued: "I say things others might ask me. Even though I know what happened, I talk it over with myself. I might ask myself questions like, 'What are you going to do next?' and 'When are you going to end it?'"

Diane was not alone. On that June morning when shafts of summer light angled into Mrs. Currier's classroom, Susie had described her writing by saying, "When I read over my first draft of "At the Beach," I thought 'How did I feel?' 'What was it like?' 'What was I thinking when I stood on that beach?' I realized probably my whole draft was like that—blah. So I wrote a new draft." Through interacting with others, Susie had learned to interact with the other in herself. Closeness and distance, pushing in and pulling back, creation and criticism: it is this combination of forces which can make writing into a powerful tool for thinking.

I once believed revision was essential to the writing process. Now I suspect it's not the revisions—the insertions, deletions and changes—which are essential. Those marks on the page are not the cutting edge of writing but only the traces of it. The cutting edge—the growing edge—of writing is the interactions between writers, their emerging texts and their developing meanings. The writer pulls in to write, then pulls back to ask, "What have I said?" "Where is this leading me?"

The interaction between writers and their writing begins long before a single word is put onto the paper. They begin when the writing is, as Robert Frost says, "a lump in the throat, a sense of wrong, a homesickness, a lovesickness."

But when words loosen themselves from the writer and lie on the page, a new distance emerges, bringing new possibilities for interaction. Frank Smith (1982) explains, "Writing separates our ideas from ourselves in a way that is easiest for us to examine, explore and develop" (p. 15). Whereas our spoken words fade away, with print we can hold our ideas in our hands, we can carry them in our pockets. We can bring them out and scrutinize them, or we can gaze admiringly at them. Writing allows us to think about our thinking.

Therefore, although many textbooks urge children to write for an audience, writers will often say, "I am my first and most important critic and reader."

"I don't think I have ever written for anybody except the other in one's self," Edmund Blunden has said, and many writers would agree.

In an article entitled, "Teaching the Other Self," Murray (1982) likens the act of writing to a conversation between two workmen muttering to each other at the workbench. "The self speaks, the other self listens and responds. The self proposes, the other self considers. The self makes, the other self evaluates. The two selves collaborate."

In my data, there seems to be an identifiable sequence to children's developing ability to conference with themselves. In classrooms where teacher:child conferences were predictable, children soon used these conferences as models for their conferences with each other. Peer conferences were in turn internalized into children's first conferences with themselves. At first, children didn't ask their own questions of their text, but instead anticipated questions their friends would ask. As six-year-old Greg said, "They'll still have questions, but at least I got rid of some of their questions."

Another first grader, Laura, wrote:

We plad a gam

and then, as if anticipating the question "What game?" she exclaimed, "Oh, no! They're going to kill me." Soon Laura had sounded out and spelled the name "Aggravation," and her page looked like this:

We plad ~~a gam~~ agoushon

Laura continued writing. This time as she printed out her lines, she muttered, "I already told you why."

Mi hol famle likes penut buttr

Across the table, another first grader chatted to himself as he forged ahead in a book called "All Abt Rbts." Finishing one page, Brad said, "And what do they eat?" Then he turned to the next page and wrote:

Rabs at cars [Rabbits eat carrots]

In second-grade classrooms, writing continued to be a dialecti-
cal process, a "continual auditing of one's meaning" (I. A.
Richards). After seven-year-old Heather reread each page of her
book, she said in a prim, matter-of-fact voice, "I'm having an
individual writing conference with myself." She continued, "On
each page I ask myself the questions the other kids would ask
me." Opening her book to page two, she said, "Here I wrote,
'I have a horse.' The kids would ask me if I ride it, so I'm going to
add, 'I ride my horse everyday unless it's raining.'"

By fourth grade, it seemed that sometimes when children
asked themselves questions, they were not only anticipating
their audience's questions, but also generating their own questions. Instead of filling in gaps in the *presentation* of a subject
alone, they were also filling in gaps in their *understanding* of it.
Gene Baro describes the writer by saying, "He told the truth in
order to see." And in time, it seemed that the children in our
study were writing not only to communicate, but also to learn.

In April of fourth grade, Susie told me she was going to write a
poem. "One time me and my father took a walk in the woods,"
she said, explaining what the poem would be about. "It was dim
and our shoes made little balls of ice that went rolling down the
hill." Then she wrote her first draft:

> The sun shone down low in the sky.
> Tiny snowballs, making go downhill.
> Sun. Beautiful, beyond hill
> Warm crisp air. My Father: wonderful,
> Nice. Liking, like me, the best
> Mine. Brightness, beauty, trees.
> Peace all around.

Afterward she had a little conference with herself. "Some of this
they may not understand . . . the part about 'My father, liking,
like me.'" Susie moved on to another draft, but before she wrote
she said, "I'm trying to think of a special word for my dad. He's
not like any other person . . ." While I watched Susie she paused,
her pen poised over the paper. It seemed she was experiencing
the dialoguing which Rebecca West has described as "communication between different parts of a person's mind."

Susie wrote several more drafts of her poem, and none of them
was quite right. Sometimes she spoke, often she was quiet. "You
can write a poem saying about things," she said once, "you can
tell about the feelings. But, like, the poem has to *be* the feelings,
not just tell them." Then Susie turned back to her page and
continued to reach for the words to convey—and to understand—
the way she felt about her father and their shared moment. She
read draft seven to Diane:

The Wonderful Walk
Walking through the woods,
Dad and I.
Not worrying,
Not today.
Not talking of troubles but of
Smooth soft sparkling snow
And bright sun going down
Sharing the beauty
The Wonderful Walk.

"*Final!*" Diane announced triumphantly, her voice ringing with such clarity that it seemed the poem was her own.

But Susie paused, unsurely, and looked it over. "No," she said, "not yet."

"What don't you like about it?" Diane asked, perplexed, then added, "I *love* it."

"I'm not sure I'm getting the exact feelings I am trying to get . . ." Susie answered. Then, as if she was still reaching for the words to capture the moment, she said, " . . . how clean, how white, and the sun shining. How good we felt."

It seemed crystal clear to me. Susie was not anticipating her friend's questions, she was not reaching for the words to convey that moment to an audience. Instead, she needed to find the right words so she could hold onto that moment for herself. She was not writing for an audience at all, but for herself. As Blunden has said, "I don't think I have ever written for anybody except the other in one's self."

21. Concept development

Researchers from Canada, Australia and Great Britain as well as the United States have visited our research site and studied our data. They've all had questions—many questions—but it was Howard Gardner who asked the simplest, most difficult question of all: "What is Susie trying to do when she writes?" he asked. "What are her goals, her concepts of good writing?"

So far in this book, I've managed to dance around Gardner's question, touching only on the edges of it, mostly staying on safer grounds. I've dealt with more overt issues: "What was the environment in which Susie learned to write?" "What did Susie *do* as she wrote? "How did these behaviors change?"

But Gardner's question has been omnipresent, for Susie's intentions were at the root of her activities. Because her writing involved an interplay of creation and criticism, her writing was propelled by concern for making meaning . . . and it was guided and shaped by concepts of good writing. Susie built and rebuilt her sense of good writing while she operated within it.

For two weeks now, I've been on the verge of plunging into the pulsing issue of Susie's concept development. I've stood on the brink of writing this chapter; and I've stood, and stood, and stood. I've cleaned my house thrice over, read more than I have in months, and written countless preparatory outlines. This morning I phoned Don Graves who had just completed a book on our study. "How's your chapter on concept development?" I asked, feigning lightness. There was a long pause on the other end of the phone. Finally Don answered, "Well, to tell the truth, I haven't gotten to it yet."

George Kelly (1955) tells the story of how Locke sat down one evening to write, before retiring to bed, the *Essay Concerning Human Understanding*. He didn't finish the essay until twenty years later. I empathize—that's how I feel about writing on concept development. The complexity of the topic is the only thing I'm sure of, and it's particularly complex when it involves older children. A six-year-old's choices in writing are apt to arise out of a single value ("It should be longer"; "It should tell more excitement"; "It shouldn't go hippity hop all over the place"), but the decisions of older children often emerge from a complex web of interacting values. Whereas a six-year-old's thinking tends to be up-front and explicit, it's not unusual for an older child to say, "This feels wrong" and then proceed into a whole chain of revisions, leaving a researcher to guess at the implicit concepts which guided his or her choices. Then, too, whereas six-year-olds attend to their writing mostly when the text (and the researcher) are on hand, this was not so for Susie. For her, the interplay of creation and criticism might continue while she was riding her bike, chatting with her mother or drifting off to sleep.

Like a detective, then, I was left searching for clues, piecing together tentative answers to Gardner's question. And now as I prepare to write on Susie's concept development, I feel like cleaning the house once more.

Documenting concept development becomes all the more difficult for me because, although every child in a classroom may have striven to achieve *focus* in their writing, *focus* might mean something quite different to one child than to another. Every writer supplies her own changing, often inarticulate meanings to "the qualities of good writing." And concept development becomes more amorphous still because these qualities do not necessarily operate as discrete values. Especially for third and fourth graders, many of the criteria of good writing cluster into hierarchical arrangements, some taking priority over others. For every child in the study, both their concepts and the organization of concepts were undergoing constant revision.

Psychologist George Kelly has helped me envision this change by suggesting the metaphor of people as scientists. When I apply Kelly's metaphor to writing development, I see children— miniature scientists—building theories of good writing, projecting them like transparent templates onto their evolving texts, then altering the texts or the theories to align one with the other. Just as researchers are guided by theoretical points-of-view, so too, when Susie wrote her drafts, they were shaped by her prior convictions about good writing. Just as researchers continually find new evidence which leads them to change their theories, so too Susie's work led her continually to refine her concept of good writing.

Concept development can be examined in terms of these overlapping, interconnected characteristics:

1. Correspondence between writing products and concept development.
2. Changes in the number of concepts in a child's repertoire.
3. Changes in the sophistication of these concepts.   ·
4. Changes in concept density (the number of concepts mentioned at any one time, in reference to a single piece of writing).

These categories are provisional ones which have been projected onto the data largely through the efforts of Rebecca Rule, who spent months studying concept development in our sixteen case-study subjects in grades one through four. But enough of house-cleaning.

It's not easy to claim definitive relationships between Susie's breakthroughs in concept development and the quality of her written products, for the quality of a piece of writing, like any art object, is debatable. Nevertheless, an interesting relationship may exist between Susie's written products and her concepts. Rule describes such a relationship, saying: "The quality of Susie's writing varies tremendously and it's not necessarily the best pieces of writing in which she makes the greatest breakthroughs in concept development. On the contrary, concept breakthroughs seem to happen on her best and on her worst pieces."

In fourth grade, Susie made tremendous breakthroughs in her concepts when she discussed the "Swinging Vines" story—which surely is not one of her best. Rule explained to me her theory about this: "It seems you have to write bad things to write good things. Often concepts develop through failures . . . in fact, the children's concepts seem to be developing no matter what their products turn out like." She added, "There's a lot of hidden concept development that goes on underground, and then when a writing topic comes up where that concept applies, the concept bursts out."

I mention Rule's hunches because they have a ring of truth for me. I suspect she's onto something and look forward to seeing future research projects which ferret out the connections between products and concepts.

I figured it was obvious—as Susie got older and more experienced, she'd develop more concepts of good writing. And indeed within the first weeks of third grade there was a dramatic leap ahead in the number of concepts which she cited. Whereas in her story about a clockmaker, Susie seemed to ask only "Is this correct?" and "What else should I add?" within just a few weeks she was suddenly aware of a large number of criteria. By November of that year, Susie was juggling one criterion against another, as is evident in this discussion of "The Big Fish."

> I was thinking of what really happened and what would fit with the real thing and look good on paper.
> I'm trying to put all the stuff that happened onto the paper. I could write a big book about it and I wanted to just put down a tiny bit . . . trying to decide what little bit to put down!

Earlier, I illustrated the new interplay of elements that had entered Susie's writing process:

September   November

But then something curious happened. After November, the number of qualities of good writing in Susie's repertoire seemed to remain constant. In "The Big Fish" story, she seemed aware of using convention, information, action, focus, tone, organization, audience, truth and correctness to build a good story . . . and in late fourth grade, she was still speaking about these and only these aspects of good writing. Although Susie had continued to gain experience as a writer, her concept development had not involved an increasing number but instead an increasing sophistication of concepts.

Looking back, I suspect the early increase in the number of Susie's concepts was not due to concept development so much as to changes in her classroom. Susie's clockmaker story was not written about a true event—therefore, she didn't ask "Is this true?" "What was the correct order in which things happened?" "Did I leave out any information?" I suspect that, had she been writing a personal narrative, she would have asked these questions of her writing. This is one reason I urge children to begin learning the writing process through personal narratives; until they know something about writing fiction, they often do not impose constraints on their make-believe stories and without constraints, they see little reason to revise. But a second change had also happened in Susie's classroom during those first few weeks. When Susie wrote the clockmaker story, she was not writing for real and responsive readers, but rather for a still unknown teacher. When she began to have real audiences, a host of new concerns entered her writing: her audience prized "action," and so Susie became concerned about choosing exciting topics. Her audience wanted their questions answered, so Susie grew concerned about providing necessary information.

What I am suggesting is that the *number* of concepts a child has in her repertoire may relate less to her concept development than to the context of her writing. When children write about topics they know well, to interested and questioning audiences, the topics and the audiences make demands on the writer which makes even first graders place higher demands on themselves. After spending months studying concept development in our case-study subjects, Rebecca Rule told me, "I have a hunch that most of the concepts are present in some simple form even with the very young writers. First graders care about information, organization, even point-of-view . . . and it's just a matter of developing sophistication in their understanding and use of these concepts."

Although Susie's writing concepts did not increase dramatically in number, they did increase in sophistication. The general trend between third and fourth grade was that concepts which Susie first regarded as single undifferentiated "Goods" became increasingly differentiated and conditional.

When Susie was eight, *action* was a goal . . . later it became a tool. She learned ways in which varying amounts of action could create different effects. Susie cautioned her friends, "You want action, but not too much action. You have to know when to put action in. If you have too much, people won't believe your story." And so it is with life. It seems so simple until we look closer, and then the Absolutes don't seem so absolute, everything becomes relative, and decisions grow harder. One of Susie's young classmates said it well: "The more you do in life, the harder it is to write. You're growing older . . . and as I grow older, I have to think about things more; I try to think about the details . . . and the writing gets harder" (Wendy Walsh, age 9).

Wendy's words hang over the desk in our research office at the University of New Hampshire. I don't know if they are more a source of comfort or of concern. Susie and her classmates were only nine, yet already their once simple goals had become complex and relative, and they'd learned that decisions aren't made by rule but by balancing priorities; that is, by making choices.

Rather than looking at each of Susie's many concepts of good writing, tracing the way her understanding of them changed, I would like to look closely at one, then, with less detail, at a sampling of others.

The changes in Susie's use of *truth* as a criterion for good writing are in some ways representative of the overall changes in understanding of elements of good writing. In early third grade, "telling the truth" was an Absolute Goal, taken literally. But when Susie tried to tell exactly what happened when she learned to fly, the resulting story was an odd one. It was as if Susie had crept over her memory-track with a magnifying glass, retelling each minute detail without any sense of the whole:

> "Susie, what are you doing?"
> "Just trying to fly."
> "Well, if you want to fly, go outside and do it, you're making too much noise."
> "But what if I start to fly and I float over to China?"
> "I wouldn't worry about that if I were you. I'll be down in the cellar if you need advice."
> "Okay Dad, I'm going out now."
> "Hey Susie, your sister wants to come too . . . so come on in."
> "Okay Dad, I'm coming in now."

Susie's dogged pursuit of an exact one-to-one rendition of the remembered events seemed to have prevented her from stepping back to create the setting (saying, for example, "my father and I were talking in the living room"), to provide background information (for example, "I was only six-years-old and determined to fly"), or to make transitions out of dialogue. Her attention was on the subject rather than on an interplay of subject/audience/text. Flower (1981) would probably call this writer-based prose; I call it retelling.

Soon Susie realized that a "true" retelling from memory was not necessarily enough. In "The Big Fish," Susie's concern for truth vied with a concern for audience and for text. "I'm trying to think of . . . what would fit with the real thing and look good on paper," she said.

Six weeks later, however, when Susie wrote "Snuggling with Daddy," her first leads were reminiscent of "Learning to Fly."

> Bang! There goes the hamper. He must be almost done with his shower. I can't wait. "Jill, make room, Dad's coming out!"
> "Nooo, I will when he comes out."
> "Well, here he comes. Hi Daddy!"

Then in later leads, Susie backed off from retelling and showed a new concern with representing. Whereas earlier in third grade Susie would probably have defended a draft of her writing, as children so often do, by saying, "But that is what really happened," by the middle of third grade she seemed to realize that truth is contained not in events alone but in her re-creation of them. She wanted to convey the whole rather than simply the parts. She brought an artistic distance to her writing. She wrote: "I snuggled deeper in the blanket. Something big was missing." Then she said, "I'm trying to figure out how, with the same feeling, I can bring my father to the sofa." She was in control; she was bringing rather than following her father to the sofa. With this new control came a new ability to distance from the exact sequence of events. Susie ended up writing: "I snuggle deeper in the blanket. I feel uneasy. Something big is missing. Then Daddy comes and lays down with me. He makes a pocket with his legs. I crawl in . . . "

A year later, in fourth grade, Susie's concern for representing the whole of the event led her not only to skip over some of the parts, but also to take poetic license with them. After writing the story about meeting her grandparents in the airport, she told me her favorite part was "true but not true."

"I liked the part when I was getting off the plane and I could tell by looking at Jill that she was as excited as me. I don't know if that happened, but I know she *was* excited and I wanted to put in that I looked at her and saw she was excited, to show how we felt . . . " Then Susie added, "It's much better now, as I read it over I almost tell the exact feelings I felt then."

Susie's understanding of truth had become quite sophisticated. Her new understanding reminded me of a quote from C. S. Lewis (1977):

> The real theme may be, and perhaps usually is, something that has no sequence to it, something other than a process and much more like a state or quality. Giantship, otherness, the desolation of Space. (p. 88)
> In life and art both . . . we are always trying to catch in our net of successive moments something that is not successive. (p. 89)

Susie had taken an important step. She had gained that sense of distance which may mark the separation from writing-as-play to writing-as-art. As Suzanne Langer wrote (1942), "Sheer self-expression requires no artistic form" (p. 215). Langer explained her point, using music as an example: "What is true of language is essential in music; music that is invented while the composer's mind is fixed on what is to be expressed is not apt to be music" (p. 240).

And so, by fourth grade, Susie's mind was no longer fixed on retelling the true events, but instead on representing the Truth of the event. The "true thing" was no longer a given. Susie had learned that she must make her own truth.

Similar changes occurred in Susie's understanding of focus. In early third grade, she and most of her classmates viewed focus as a quality which belonged to their subject rather than to their treatment of a subject. They interpreted focus as "having to choose one tiny thing to write about," and many children went to ridiculous lengths to reduce their topics, often shrinking out all possibility for combining contrasts into a single piece, or for showing the evolution of their subject. It was not unusual, for example, for a child to begin his first draft with his pride over his tankful of fish and proceed from there to show dismay as day-after-day he would find another fish lying belly-up on the water's surface . . . and for the story to be reduced, draft-by-draft, until the final piece was an ineffective little story about a single fish, lying belly-up in the water.

But in time, Susie and many of her classmates realized that focus, like truth, was not an Absolute Goal, nor did it reside in the subject as much as in their treatment of the subject. By late fourth grade, Susie once again saw that she had the option to write about a chain of events, or about different aspects of a topic. In her glacier report, for example, Susie said, "You can tell different things about your topic, not just one thing. Like I put subtitles: the beginning of the glacier, the making of mountains, how glaciers melt . . . "

But now that focus was *made* rather than found, Susie had to develop ways to create unity, or thematic focus, in her pieces. Some concepts became more important. For example, she showed a new concern for building cohesion into her stories. And she used poetic license—small untruths—to weave the threads of each of her stories into a single fabric. In the piece about meeting her grandparents, Susie realized that all of a sudden, midway into it, she mentioned her mother's friend. Apparently the woman had been with Susie and her family all along, but hadn't been brought into the story until this late point. So Susie crossed out all the references to the woman, explaining, "I didn't have her before in the story, so she can't just come in now." But when Susie noticed that her sister too hadn't entered the story until very late, she decided to write another draft. "See, in draft 1, Jill was just suddenly there. So I'll put her in from the beginning."

Susie also used feelings—or mood—to weave the parts of her stories into a cohesive whole. In "Snuggling with My Father," she was able to sacrifice telling every little event, in sequence, so long as she infused the story with a single feeling. And in a later story about a campfire, the one in which Susie had been troubled by changes in tone and had said, "Up here has a different tone, explaining, than down here," it almost seemed that Susie's concern for cohesion and for mood were half-steps toward an understanding of thematic focus.

Over the course of the two-year study, Susie's understanding of good endings—like her understanding of other concepts of good writing—changed from a rigid sense of The Right Way to an awareness of options. In early third grade, Susie was clear about endings: "They shouldn't just go off," she said, and indeed, her endings reminded me of a little knot, tied onto the end of each of her pieces:

Learning to Fly   The next day I planned to try again and just keep on doing it until I flew. So I tried and tried and I'm still trying.

Batting Is Fun   But when I play baseball with my sister I hit pop-flies . . . and I get out. But I'm still very proud of my batting.

The Big Fish   . . . and I finally caught a big fish and I was satisfied. Wouldn't you be?

A year later, when Susie wrote about falling out of a bunkbed, she said, "I usually have a little line to end it, like 'I'll never sleep in that bunk bed again!'" Then she said, "I think, for a change, I won't put that in." Instead she ended the piece with her mother consoling her. For a while, Susie tended to end her stories with either a "little line" or with going to bed, arriving home, reaching her destination . . . some event which would bring closure to the piece. But at the end of fourth grade she realized her options were broader still. "Endings can leave them hanging," she said. "Usually they don't, but they can." Once again, Susie had learned there are no hard and fast rules, and that the rightness of any choice depends on a multitude of factors.

Earlier in this book, we saw Susie's writing process move from a linear sequence of steps toward a vibration of processes. By late fourth grade, the only diagram of the writing process which seemed applicable to Susie's process is the one Pulitzer Prize winning writer Donald M. Murray has drawn:

This diagram, I think, not only illustrates Susie's writing process, but also the way in which the desire to write with detail vies with a desire for conciseness; the way an interest in answering her reader's questions competes with an interest in poetic sounding language. Whereas in early third grade (and, I suspect, even more so in first and second grade), Susie probably considered these qualities of writing one at a time, by fourth grade she seemed to be able to juggle multiple criteria, and her writing became a vibration of simultaneous, often competing, criteria. Researcher Rule, who refers to this as an increasing density of concepts, points out that it's telling to realize that when Susie talked about a piece of writing in early third grade, she usually referred to two or three concepts; by fourth grade, within a single bit of talk about a single piece of writing, she often mentioned between seven and ten.

Flower (1981) likens the writer to "a very busy switchboard operator trying to juggle a number of demands on her attention and constraints on what she can do." Flower continues, saying, "As a dynamic process, writing is the act of dealing with an excessive number of simultaneous demands or constraints." Her observations match my own.

Arnheim (1969) refers to the same "organization of tensions" in this important passage:

> The artist is constantly faced with the problem of how to develop the part in terms of the whole. . . . The artist works out partial entities, acting upon each other dialectically. An interplay of interferences, modifications, restrictions and compensations leads gradually to the unity of and complexity of the total composition. . . . The total result, obtained through successive operations, presents itself as a marvel of organized complexity.

Just as Susie's process became, in time, less systematic and packaged so too her sense of the components of good writing became less absolute, less discrete. "This feels wrong," she'd say. She didn't elaborate with reasons, for her once clear distinctions between good and bad had become more tentative. Susie's sense of good writing was no longer a preset list of absolute values. "It's better now," she'd say. "I can tell because I listen to it, and I look it over. It just feels better."

22. Reading-writing connections

They say it's the nature of case-study research that only as a project ends does it become clear what might have been. They tell me I should feel good about my regrets, about my "if only I'd . . ." feelings, that I should write them up—not as a "Regrets Column," but as "Suggestions for Future Research." And I suppose I can forgive myself for not getting baseline data onto videotape, or watching Craig as closely as Susie, or documenting my informal discussions with the teachers. But it was not out of ignorance that I ignored the reading-writing connection. It was out of spite.

For years, I'd watched teachers spend two hours a day on the teaching of reading, and barely any time on the teaching of writing. Those precious morning hours—prime time, we called them—inevitably went to reading and mathematics. If there was any writing at all, it was done just before the Halloween party, when the film projector broke down, or during the last minutes before afternoon bus call. Then, too, as a teacher I'd seen that each year the language arts budget went almost exclusively for reading textbooks and kits. There never seemed to be money left over for postage stamps, italic pens, or book-binding supplies. Don Graves, I found, shared my dismay at the imbalance between the basics. Don had just completed a study funded by the Ford Foundation on the status of writing in our country. These were some of his findings (1976):

> A review of public educational investment at all levels showed that for every dollar spent on the teaching of writing, a hundred or more are spent on the teaching of reading.
>
> A random survey of thirty six universities which prepare teachers showed that 169 courses were offered in reading, 30 in children's literature . . . and only 2 focused on the teaching of writing.

Although both Don and I had backgrounds in reading, we'd come to view reading as our nation's neurosis. We agreed with Moffett:

> Reading . . . has swelled out of reasonable proportions, to its detriment as well as to the detriment of other activities. . . . It

crowds out those very activities that it desperately needs. It dominates the curriculum, at the expense of itself. (1973, p. 18)

In retrospect, I think it was because I was angry at reading that I acted as if writing and reading were separate, even competing processes. Writing I saw as active and expressive, reading as passive and receptive. Because our research was on writing, I didn't make a point of documenting the interface between reading and writing. I assumed they were each based on separate skills. Of course, I was wrong. More wrong even than I secretly realized.

I was wrong, first, because there was no way I could watch writing without watching reading. While composing, children read continually. They read to savor the sounds of their language, they read to see what they had written, they read to regain momentum, they read to reorient themselves, they read to avoid writing. They read to find gaps in their work, they read to evaluate whether the piece was working, they read to edit. And they read to share the work of their hands. A research colleague counted as one six-year-old reread his work twenty-seven times before he'd finished writing one sentence. Another researcher who has examined our data (1982) calculates that some children spend as much as thirty percent of their writing time reading.

Then too, I was wrong because even when children weren't reading, they were using and developing skills which are traditionally assigned to the domain of reading. As Susie and her classmates wrote, rewrote and conferenced, they selected and reselected their main ideas, organized their supporting details, adjusted and defended their sequence. They reached toward inference, they discovered cause and effect, they developed and challenged conclusions. In a sense, everything that happened during writing time related to skills which are traditionally viewed as reading skills.

Consider Birger, who told me, "In every story I write, I'm always thinking, 'is this one story?' 'Is this two stories?' " Birger wanted to give me an example. "Like in one story, I was going to write about getting twenty cents worth of bottles adding up to a dollar, but my bike got stuck in a wheat field and I dropped the bottle story and stayed with the wheat." Birger would have been surprised to hear that he was developing a skill which is usually taught through reading kits and workbooks. Like Birger, first- and second-grade writers searched for their main idea. Some tried hard to write titles which matched their stories; others divided their writing into chapters and tried to make the chapters "go together."

Because the six-year-olds wrote on pages stapled together into a crude sort of book, usually putting just a few lines on each page,

these children often reordered their statements, thereby developing the reading skill of sequence. Once I watched six-year-old
Sharon listen to her classmate's story, "My Trip to the Football
Game." It wound its way back and forth between the bus ride:
     There were over fifty buses
and the game:
     The Patriots and the Jets played. The score was 55 to 21.
then back to the bus:
     There was a bathroom on the bus
and then to the game again:
     We saw a man with a pumpkin on his head. The policeman made
     us throw our coke in the garbage.
When Greg finished reading his story, Sharon shook her head
and said firmly, "It wasn't about one thing, Greg. It went hippity-
hop from one thing to the next. . . . It's like you went to sleep
and had a crazy dream." With the teacher's and Sharon's
help, Greg reconstructed the day's events—and the book—in
logical sequence.

During writing time, children also learned to read texts in
search of unanswered questions, lapses in logic, and missing information. In Mrs. Currier's room, I watched Jeremy read Diane's
second draft of "Falling into the River." He reread it several
times, then said, "Di, I gotta question about this part."

     I landed in the water with a big splash, "Wendy," I yelled, "get
     me out of here!"
     Wendy came giggling from behind a tree. She pulled and pulled
     and tried to get me out of it. Then SPLASH. She fell on top of me.
     She crawled out of the water and started pulling again. This time I
     came loose from the water and got hauled to shore.

"What exactly made you stick?" Jeremy asked. Poor Jeremy; his
question had been a serious one, but it struck both Diane and me
as terribly funny. Finally Diane regained composure enough to
answer.

"Well," she said, blushing. "It's hard to explain; it's like, well,
the water was pushing me down." And she sprawled herself
onto the floor, trying with her hands to illustrate the effect of the
water current. The entire episode was enormous fun for the
children—they would have been startled to hear they'd been
drilling each other on reading comprehension!

Children not only searched for gaps in each other's texts, but
they also examined their own. Seven-year-old Greg announced
to me, "When I read my stories, sometimes I see that my brilliant
ideas turn out to be a disaster." I asked what he meant. For an

answer, the youngster opened his homemade book to a marked page and read,

I looked at my father's collections. After that we left.

"See, it's a disaster," Greg said. "It should go in the trash can. It goes wicked fast through it, but it doesn't tell what we saw in the collections." Then Greg took hold of his pencil and, with arrows and cross-outs, began to repair the page. After a few minutes he said, "It's better now."

I looked at my father's collections. I saw buttons, coins, stamps, spirals that my father collected.

"I went over it and thought of all the questions I could get out," Greg said. "The collections: what are they? what kinds of collections? The kids will have questions still, but less than they would have." Greg added, "At least I got rid of some of the questions."

On every page of my observational notes, there are more anecdotes like these. And every time I go into classrooms now where writers are revising and conferring on their work, I am again reminded that writing and reading are inseparable. A few weeks ago I brought Professor Bernice Cullinan, a leading figure in the field of children's literature, to visit writing process classrooms in New York City. It was good for me to see writer-readers through her eyes, for everywhere she turned, she saw more reading. In most of the classrooms, children had learned that after listening to a friend's story in peer conference, the first task was to reconstruct what they had learned from it. And so we watched first-grade writers, with text in hand, listening as a friend recited their stories, following along in the text to be sure no details had been forgotten and no information had been misconstrued. What a sociable way to practice recall skills!

Then too, Dr. Cullinan and I watched as a six-year-old sounded out *tuxedo*. He worked with the word for several minutes, putting letters onto his page, reading them back, asking a friend for help with the /u/ sound, rereading his letters and again isolating and repeating the sounds he needed. The classroom teacher joined us as we watched. "No workbook could ever ask a first grader to do this much drill on sounds," she said, "but my writers do it all the time." When youngsters build tree forts or block structures, they surprise us with their willingness to sustain work for many hours, even days. So too when children build their own texts, they break the child labor laws.

Yes, I was wrong to view the two processes of reading and writing as separate. Wrong because writing involves reading, and because it reinforces and develops skills traditionally viewed as reading skills. And I was also wrong because writing can generate a stance toward reading which, regretfully, is rarely conveyed through reading programs. When children are makers of reading, they gain a sense of ownership over their reading. As we've seen again and again, owners are different from tenants.

So often in our efforts to teach youngsters to respect books and to read "correctly," we've taken reading out of children's hands. Reading has become less like romping about in one's own backyard and more like those stifled, pained visits to a grandparent's house. Youngsters are taught to be polite guests; they're not to ask rude questions, to blurt out their uninformed opinions. Young readers are to be seen and not heard. In most reading programs, there's rarely an opportunity for children to ask questions of a text. Instead, questions are prewritten, and they are not directed at the text at all, but at the reader. Children, well schooled in detecting their teacher's wishes and in decoding the messages implicit in our methods, have probably gotten messages like these from our reading programs:

> Texts are to be respected and remembered. It's your fault if you do not recall what was said.
> The printed word is final, and unquestionable.
> If you read well, the text should mean the same thing to you as it means to me.
> These texts have been written by very great people. You are just a child and not in a position to pass judgment on your superiors.

No wonder we mistakenly view reading as a passive and receptive act—the reading we teach in our schools often verges on being just that! In an important and recent article on critical reading, Newkirk (1982) suggests that too often our reading programs are geared toward teaching children deference rather than critical thinking:

> Even students who can accomplish the important comprehension tasks such as locating the main idea, summarizing and drawing inferences are controlled by the written language if they must accept the writing on its own terms, if they lack the power to question the integrity of the texts before them. Lacking this power, they are only deferentially literate; they are polite readers. Like good guests, they do not ask impertinent questions.

One of the greatest contributions writing can make to reading is to demythologize the printed word. I refer again to Newkirk (1982):

> All of us, to some degree, stand in awe of written language. . . . Any reading program must acknowledge this potential of written language to intimidate, to bully the reader into submission. (p. 1)
> Writing programs can make texts less imposing. By creating

their own texts, students can begin to view written language as the result of human choices and not as something fixed and authoritative. (p. 2)

Newkirk's observations strike home for me. My writing and research have certainly made me a more cautious and critical consumer of research. The change probably comes, in part, because I have a research base against which to test what I read, asking, "Does this match what I know?" But I think the change comes also from a more humble reason. I know that behind my own texts there is an emperor with no clothes on. I know, as no one else could, the gaps in this text, the compromises I have made, the goals I haven't met. And so now I view the rows of books and journals on my shelves a little differently. They are less imposing to me, they seem less final and complete. I can see the writer behind the text.

Seven-year-old Greg seems to have learned the same thing. He said it this way:

Before I ever wrote a book, I used to think there was a big machine, and they typed a title and then the machine went until the book was done.

Now I look at a book and I know a guy wrote it and it's been his project for a long time. After the guy writes it, he probably thinks of questions people will ask him and revises it like I do, and xeroxes it to read to about six editors. Then he fixes it up, like how they say.

Greg and I are both learning how reading is made. And we both read differently because we have an insider's view on reading.

When writers question a text, they do not only question it critically, to evaluate whether it works. They also examine it as fellow craftsmen, asking, "I wonder why the writer chose the lead he did?" or "I wonder if these characters come from the author's life?" Because writers are makers of reading, they have a reason to look closely at a text. Because I am in the midst of buying a car, I've suddenly developed a new interest in the ever-present cars which traverse my world each day. I notice the differences between the Datsun and the Toyota, and wonder whether front-wheel drive is as good as four-wheel drive. Similarly, when children view themselves as authors, they approach texts with the consciousness of "I am one who needs to know how texts are made." Writing gives them a new reason to connect with reading. Birger came into school one morning, saying, "Last night I read a book called *And Then Again, Maybe I Won't*. I can't figure out why he called it that—the author only used those words one time in that whole book, and it was at the end."

Susie often mentioned descriptions she found in her reading

books, reminding me of V.S. Pritchett's comment, "I read for the pleasure of learning how to write."

Over the last few months, Susie's fourth-grade teacher and other writing process teachers with whom I've worked have been telling me they're extending their students' interest in reading by encouraging them to hold peer conferences in reading, just as they do in writing. "The questions are almost the same," the teachers tell me, "and the more children interact with their reading, the better they do in their writing." These are some of the questions the children may be asking in reading conferences:

About the Lead
- Does the author make me want to read on? How does the author do this?
- How's this lead like the ones I've been writing? How's it different?
- When I read the lead, what do I expect will follow in the book?
- Does the book begin at the beginning of the story, or does it begin somewhere else, like in a flashback?

About the Characters
- Which of the characters seems most real? Why?
- What sections of the book especially helped me to know the characters? Can I learn from these sections?
- What makes some of the characters work better than others?
- Where does the author tell me about the character? Where are they shown rather than told about?
- How do the characters change through the story?

About the Point-of-View
- Who tells the story?
- Why might the author have decided to do it this way?
- How else might it have been done?
- Does this way work?
- What can I learn from the author's treatment of point of view?

About the Plot
- Can I map the sequence of events?
- Is this story mostly events, or mostly characters, or what?
- How does the writer skip forward in time? Backward?
- How does the writer make things speed up or slow down?

About the Ending
- Does the ending relate back to the beginning?
- Is it a summing-up ending? Should there be one?
- Can I put the book down now . . . does it feel like *The End*?

I confess, when Mrs. Currier told me about the new trade books she has ordered for her classroom, about her reading conferences and the bridges she and the children are building between reading and writing, I wanted to say, "Why, oh why didn't you do all that when I was there to document it?" But of course I cannot blame her for being slow to see the connections between reading and writing. I, too, was slow to learn what the children were showing me.

23. Reading, writing and a glacier report

The more I delve into children's writing, the more I want to study the connections between reading and writing. The interface between them, I believe, is the research territory of the future. I'm not surprised that even before final reports were in from our study, Graves had begun a follow-up project, examining the connections between reading and writing. His study, like most of the research relating reading and writing processes, will focus on four- to six-year-old children. This is not surprising. Progress is rapid for these little ones, and both reading and writing are externalized so much that they're easy to see, to videotape, to document. But there is another territory which needs to be explored. What are the links between reading and writing for children who can already decode and encode words? What are the relationships between reading and writing for youngsters like Susie, Birger, Craig and Diane?

I have a hunch that if we replayed Susie's third- and fourth-grade years, we'd find strong similarities between her reading and writing processes. When Susie was a pixielike eight-year-old, both the products and the process of her writing resembled a chain: $X \rightarrow X \rightarrow X \rightarrow X$. There was relatively little back and forth movement, and there was little ability to distance from a text, to ask questions of it. Unless Susie stumbled over a troublesome spelling, her attention tended to follow her pencil steadily down the page until The End, whereupon writing was over. This seemed typical for third-grade writers who'd gained fluency with print yet didn't understand the craft of writing. I suspect that this third-grade plateau characterizes reading development as well as writing development. Once young readers gain fluency, their reading probably resembles Susie's chainlike writing. Their eyes, like Susie's hand, move forward, one word at a time—the next, the next, the next—until The End, whereupon reading is over. The tragedy is that too often reading development, like writing development, doesn't move beyond this point.

When I read, I ask questions, I push forward and backward. "What does this imply about that earlier passage?" "How do these parts connect?" "Do I agree?" "Have I met this character before in this story?" I manipulate the text in order to build meaning. Sometimes the interplay of creation and criticism happens line by line, sometimes the momentum of one force overtakes the other for a while, but both remain. The craft of reading, like the crafts of writing, science and art, involves an interplay of forces, a dialogue of perspectives.

We've seen this interactive quality develop in Susie's writing, but did it carry over into her reading? I suspect it did. While curricula are divided into separate subjects, people are not. But my suspicions are based not only on common sense, but also on a glimpse I was given, late in her fourth-grade year, of Susie's reading. It was Susie's first social studies report which provided me with this window onto her reading. The evolution of that report is a story worth telling, and so in this chapter, my discussion of her reading will be embedded in a larger discussion of her first serious expedition into content-area writing.

Every spring for years and years, the fourth graders at Atkinson Elementary School have written "New Hampshire State Reports." These reports have become a tradition—even the dittoed guide sheets enumerating items to be included are tradition. And so I was surprised when Mrs. Currier mentioned over lunch that she'd been rethinking the state reports. "They seem to go against everything we've been teaching," she said. When I looked over the guide sheets, I agreed. How could children write with detail, focus and voice if they were required to tell about the state bird, flower, rivers, mountains, minerals, products and history? How could children conference, draft and revise if the only feedback they received was an autopsy on the finished work?

That spring at Atkinson Elementary School, traditions were broken . . . and begun. It started one morning in early March when the air smelled like spring and the playground was dotted with jackets and hats. Mrs. Currier gathered her children together to build a flow chart of "Things about New Hampshire." From this, the children chose topics they cared about for their reports: the white-tailed deer, granite quarries, the Merrimack River. Susie chose glaciers.

That was Friday. On Monday we were dismayed to find children coming to school with reams of notes and, in some instances, finished reports. Following tradition, they'd gone to the town library on Saturday morning and copied the encyclopedia. They felt proud of themselves; grown up, as if they'd gone through initiation rites, as perhaps they had. Debbie later told me: "I didn't know how to do it; I had lumps in my throat, butterflies in my stomach. This was the first time I'd done a *real report*. They said, 'put down the important facts,' so I did, out of the encyclopedia: people, places, dates, Indians and wars."

The children's weekend efforts became a lesson for Mrs. Currier. Clearly she'd have to begin again, this time helping students transfer the writing process into report writing. Her first step was to put content-area writing into a time slot which had once been reserved for writing process. "It's no different," she assured the children. And indeed, writing was still stored in folders, only now the front covers had a space for *Bibliography*, and the back covers for *Vocabulary Words*. Writing time still began with a mini-lesson, only now the nutshell lessons were on finding resource material, bibliographies, mapping and note-taking.

In one of these mini-lessons, Mrs. Currier asked children to pretend they were each researching bird migration, and together the class went through the steps of selecting resource material and taking notes. Mrs. Currier had collected books on the topic, including a primary-level book and an encyclopedia. "Which would you read first?" she asked and in the discussion which ensued, children learned to read simpler books first, gaining a grasp of their subjects before they tackled denser texts. Then Mrs. Currier suggested students leaf through the book, becoming familiar with the topic. After that the class brainstormed questions they hoped to answer, filling the blackboard with these. From this collection, each student—and the teacher—selected a few questions. While the teacher wrote her questions on top of sections of the blackboard, the students put theirs on top of sheets of yellow paper. "The next thing we do is we read until our heads are full," Mrs. Currier told the class. After a few minutes of reading out loud from the primary-level book, she stopped and the class recounted what they'd learned, then filed relevant bits of information under the appropriate question-headings.

With this lesson behind her, Susie began her research on glaciers. "My father went to the library and got some books," she said, "and at home I started reading them. I wanted to find some questions that were interesting."

I remember observing children read reference books; invariably it seemed they begin at the first page and read along until they grow tired. And so I was surprised by Susie's description of the reading she did at home.

> In my book there are different subtitles and I flipped through them until I found one that was interesting. Sometimes you have to read two parts to understand one, so I read them both and tried to see if it was a good and important part.
>
> I read "How Geologists Study" and my father said I could use

that as a question for my report or not; it was up to me. So I called up Diane and we talked and decided it wasn't that good of an idea. It's not that much about glaciers.

Clearly, Susie was reading with a purpose, with a selective eye, steering her way through the text rather than being bound to a straight-forward linear progression. I was amazed at the apparent parallels between her writing and her reading, but Susie meanwhile continued to chatter away, oblivious to my response.

So then I kept on reading and I decided to do a part on ice crystals so I wrote a note on the top of the page to remember to do that. I was going to take notes on the melting of the glacier after I did the crystals, but I am doing the crystals first and I'll rearrange my notes after.

Reading, for Susie, was far from passive. Rather than simply receiving a text, Susie was actively forming structures, building and shaping her meaning. Her reading was inseparable from learning. "Whatever else learning may be," Gordon Allport wisely commented, "it is clearly a disposition to form structures." By late fourth grade, that "disposition to form structures" had become second nature for Susie.

In school, as Susie continued to gather and organize information about glaciers, she moved easily between reading and writing. To me it seemed she relied all the while on strategies and thinking skills I'd observed in her writing. Whereas I'd often watched her planning ahead in her writing, now I watched as she surveyed the text before her, read, made predictions and organized her attack. The executive function which had given her flexibility and control in writing seemed crucial to her reading, for as she proceeded through books, she monitored and directed her processes, shuttling between reading/rereading/planning/recalling/questioning/reading/talking/writing . . .

I remember one morning watching Susie "read" about glaciers. She began by scanning five pages of notes she'd collected. Each of the pages represented a different subtopic:

Where do glaciers come from?
Are they going to be around a lot again?
How many are left?
Where did they start forming?
Other?

Susie put down her notes and headed to the bookshelf at the back of the classroom. She found a reference book, searched through it, then returned that book to the shelf. She located a second book, and this time Susie returned with it to her desk. Putting on her newly acquired glasses, Susie began to look over the book.

Page 268 must have contained what she was looking for—Susie read the entire page, slowly. Then she added to her notes:

Piedmont glaciers are rare. They are valley glaciers that move onto a plain. Alaska has a piedmont.

"I'm not sure what information I should get next," Susie mused. "Should I look up the ice age—they said so in the book, that it relates." And so, with me on her trail, Susie headed off for the school library, found several books and used the index in one to locate a section on the ice age. Again she returned to her desk. This time when she looked up from reading, she said to Diane, "I gotta find something on the map, want to help?" And so the two girls pulled the United States wall map down from its roller, and chatted as they surveyed it. When Susie returned, she explained to me, "I wanted to see where the Great Lakes are and I am going to add a little about them, because the glaciers formed them." Because she couldn't find an appropriate place in her notes to file the new information, Susie added a new category:

What types of things did the glaciers form? One very popular place they made were the great lakes. Glaciers must have been around Michigan, Wisconsin and Minnesota to form the Great Lakes. I never knew how big lakes were made. The glaciers also built mountains along side of them as they flowed along where they had been . . .

Susie returned to her reading. After five minutes, she added another category to her notes, this time putting just the page number of the reference book beside the heading. "If I want to do detailed stuff later, I can remember the page." Again Susie read, and again she returned to her notes. She scanned each page of them, inserting new bits of information here and there throughout them, and occasionally crossing out sections which didn't fit. Mostly she worked quietly, but at one point she said, "I was thinking in the first section I didn't explain what a glacier is so people know—I'm telling how it melts without telling what it is."

In this sort of way, Susie continued reading and writing for another fifteen minutes. Finally, she leaned back in her chair. "I might start a draft now and it'll help me decide what should go first." But writing workshop was over for that day, and Susie had yet to learn what was in store for her.

During our lunch times, Mrs. Currier and I had kept each other updated on the children's progress. Although Susie was just approaching her first draft, others were well into theirs. That morning Mrs. Currier brought the drafts to lunch and bemoaned, "So many are *still* not writing in their own words!" She read sections to me and as we talked, we realized the children didn't know what it meant to write in their own words. They thought they were doing just that.

For example, whereas Craig's book had said "The dappled fawn lay in the leaves," he'd proudly written it, "The *spotted* fawn lay in the leaves." Even Birger had said to me, "I decided to make it in my own words so I found out what the words I didn't know meant. I looked it up in a dictionary. Now I'm putting it into my own words, not using the big words." As Mrs. Currier and I read over the papers and reflected on what the children were telling us, we realized what was missing: that nebulous, all important quality writers call "voice."

The next morning began with a class meeting. "We've always said that in order to write well, writers need to know and care about their subjects," Mrs. Currier began. "That's true for report writing, too. It's not enough to read two books and then write them up. You have to feel like an expert on your topic." To give children this sense of personal authority, she suggested they teach each other what they knew. This was a new form of peer conferencing, and so she suggested the class try it as a group first.

Birger, a little embarrassed and very pleased, went to the front of the classroom and taught his classmates about squirrels. He described their food, enemies and appearance, but the thing which most intrigued his classmates was a curious statement he made about squirrels squeaking when they're too cold. When Birger's lecture was finished, he called on children for questions:

Diane: Does the squirrel squeak when he's sleeping?
Birger: Only if his body temperature goes below 40 degrees and that saves his life.
Diane: He automatically squeaks?
Birger: Yeah.
Nicole: Where did you get your information from, one book?
Birger: The first part was from a little encyclopedia and the middle from *Young Wildlife*.
Wendy: Do you think when he squeaks it is a natural instinct?
Birger: They didn't say . . .
Brad: How does the squeak make the body temperature go up?
Birger: I'm not sure. I'll find out.

Soon the children had divided into clusters and were teaching each other what they knew. On the rug in the library area, Amy, the class artist, told Susie and Diane about the red fox. "He is red and has a white chin and black behind the ears and on the feet. In the winter, you know how dogs have pads on their feet? Well, in the winter the fox have deep soft fur on their feet and in the cold, they take their soft tails and wrap around them."

Diane, already an expert on the mating habits of beavers,

seemed unappreciative of Amy's description. Getting right to the point, she asked, "How do they mate?"

"They mate for life. They just pick any fox that comes along . . . the babies are called kits."

"Baby beavers are called the same thing," Diane responded and for a while Susie listened while her friends compared animals.

When it was Susie's turn, she explained glaciers briefly, then asked for questions. Because Diane's interest in mating habits wasn't applicable to this topic, Amy led the questioning: "How do scientists tell how old the glacier is?" she wanted to know.

"It's like the rings of a tree. Every year the snow on top gets dirty so it forms layers," Susie answered.

"How do the glaciers move along?"

Susie responded, "By pressure, pushing it out," but she wasn't satisfied with her answer. The next day before school she told her friends, "I was talking with my father about how the glaciers move and my father said it's the great weight, it's just like a river. The top moves first. When I write I may tell that it's like a river, and they'll get an idea what it's like."

As well as giving children *voice* over their information, these peer conferences were providing a time for rehearsal. Listen to Craig's discussion of his topic:

> I'm going to write, "A group of white-tailed deer are in a group, the mother leaves and she sits down" and then I'm going to say, "she can feel some kicks. She decides to rest."
>
> Then I'll have a new paragraph and say that she goes to sleep to rest and she wakes up in her napping and she has a fawn.
>
> Then I'll tell how, in a new paragraph, it is like the fawn's first time trying to stand up. I didn't read about that in a book.
>
> In a book I read the first time she, the mother, has *one* fawn and then the next time she has *twins*. And usually when she has had a baby, I didn't really find it out, but I guess they don't have a father. I never read about the babies' father in a book and I was wondering.
>
> I know the white-tailed buck takes one doe, then maybe three weeks later he'll take another. He's not like most deer with lots of girls, he only takes one at a time.

After a few days of teaching each other their topics, Mrs. Currier made another suggestion. She asked children to clear their desks of all their notes and to take out a single sheet of yellow paper. "Try writing some leads, and then a draft, *without looking at your notes*. Later you can go back and insert missing information, or if this doesn't work you can later write a draft from your notes."

Although initially there were groans of resistance, children quickly realized that with work, their leads could get much better. Melissa turned her report on Celia Thaxter into a first-person narrative:

> The boat started with a sputter as I, Celia Thaxter, and my family left for the Isles of Shoals. . . . I couldn't wait to see the island we would live on. Nearer and nearer we came until . . .
>
> —Melissa

These are two other leads used by the children:

> It's very easy to find mica in your front yard because it's very shiny, and when the sun shines, it glitters. When you are looking for mica you won't find it alone. There is mica in other rocks, like granite.
>
> —Vinny

> The Merrimack River, which winds its way down from the mountain, is seriously polluted by the time it reaches Southern New Hampshire. Why?
>
> —Kenny

But far more important than the quality of the writing was the children's new investment in it. "It's mine," they'd say, "It's not like I could copy this from a book."

Leads led to first drafts. This is Susie's first draft, abandoned midway:

After reading draft 1 several times and confering with a friend, Susie decided to write a second draft, focusing on just one kind of glacier. She wrote draft 2, reread it, fiddled with her word choice and filled her margins with inserts and notes to herself. One note read: "Sue, remember. Put how glaciers start moving."

She inserted an odd mark (7) in her text, and made a similar mark in the margin—all for the purpose of changing "Something amazing happened" to read "Something amazing starts to form."

On the second page of this draft, a different code (9) was used for this insert: "After the glacier starts melting it might leave behind rivers of the melted glacier or it might leave a lake behind." Her draft soon became well-marked.

It was at this point that Susie decided to section her piece with subtitles, and so she wrote a third draft.

Page 1

After 18yrs of March 26, 1480

Susie Sible

0 Snow after the snow snow fell
the snow packed down
and turned to ice

The Beginning Of A Glac

What is a glacier

Way up in the cold Northern regions, snow falls. More and more snow falls. After many many years something amazing starts to form. So much snow fell and turned to ice. The ice got so heavy and big it actually began pushing and sliding itself along. The great weight of it actually made it This huge ice chunk starts creeping down in a Valley. That is probably how this glacier got its name. Its name is the Valley glacier. Other glaciers are the Continental glacier and the Piedmont glacier. This glaciers name is the plateau Valley Glacier.

Making Mountains

As the Valley glacier moves along it pushes dirt and rock from the sides of it. These dirt mounds form mountains. It would take a long, long time to form mountains because glaciers move along only about seven hundred to a thousand feet a year! That's not even a mile! How they melt

How glaciers they melt

Page ②

⊕ freezing cold

But if it was cold not much ~~melting~~ There was a It was warm ~~not~~ lots of melting will take place.

The ~~melting~~ of a Valley glacier is done at the end of a glacier not at the beginning. The ~~beginning~~ of a glacier is where the glacier get formed, in the North. In the North it is mostly cold. ~~so~~ Thats why it melts at ~~the~~ end. How much ~~melt~~ melts in the middle depends on the weather in that season. If, in that season there ~~was~~ ~~hot Summer~~ and ~~that a~~ winter not too cold with not much snow lots of ~~melting~~ will take place ~~in the middle~~ But, if there was a cool summer then a winter with lots of snow not very much melting will happen. I think it is interesting ~~that~~ different spots on the glacier can be different temptures. When glaciers cover a spot then melt away they may leave a lake or river buried or melted water ~~which glacier's left behind~~

Studying the glaciers

Geologists spend a lot of time studying different things about the glacier. To study

Page ③   3/31/80

Susan Sible   ~~blow~~ or get scraped up

the glacier they have to ~~a~~ camp on the glacier ~~which they do.~~ There is one thing they study that I think is very interesting. Each year it snows on the glacier. After it snows dirt and dust ~~to~~ form a light covering on the snow. Then the next year more snow falls and again the dirt comes over it. Geologists go down in deep holes they cut in the glacier. When they do they see different layers. Because they see the clean white snow then the dust dirt layers It's like looking at the rings on a tree stump to see how old it is except the geologists look to see how much snow fell each year. I would be hard work but It might be fun to study to be a geologist and study a glacier what glaciers left behind

Do you know how the Great Lakes were made? They were made by glaciers. Probably when the glaciers started melting they left huge pools of water behind them. I really never knew how lakes such as the Great Lakes were made. Did you?

After again refining and editing, Susie wrote a final draft, the proud result of three weeks of writing—and of reading.

Susie S. Ve

The Beginning Of A Glacier

In the cold northern regions, snow falls. More and more snow falls. After many, many years, something amazing starts to form. So much snow fell and turned to ice the ice got so heavy and big the great weight of it began pushing itself along. This huge ice chunk starts creeping into a valley. That is probably how this glacier got its name. Other glaciers are the Continental and the Piedmont glaciers. But this glacier's name is the Valley glacier.

Making Mountains

As the Valley glacier moves along it pushes dirt and rock out from the sides of it. These huge mounds of dirt and rock form mountains. It would take a long time to make mountains because glaciers travel only about seven hundred to a thousand feet a year. Thats not even a mile!

Melting Away

The melting of a glacier is done at the end of a glacier not at the beginning. The beginning of a glacier is where the glacier was formed in the north. In the north it is mostly cold. Thats why it melts at the end. In the middle of a glacier it will melt. How much it melts all depends on the weather of that year. If it was a mild, and warm lots of melting will take place. But if it was cold and stormy not as much melting will happen in the middle. When glaciers cover a spot then melt away a lake or river might be where the glacier was. The river or lake is water that melted from the glacier.

What Glaciers Left Behind

Do you know how the Great Lakes were made? They were made by glaciers. Probably when the glaciers started melting they left huge pools of water behind them. I really never knew how big lakes such as the Great Lakes were made. Did you?

24. Lessons from children

"**S**he's coming," Craig called as he raced back to his place in the circle. His classmates echoed the warning. "She's coming," they whispered. "Mrs. Howard is coming!"

"Children, get ready," Mrs. Currier added, but her comment was needless for the children were already sitting a little taller and nudging each other to straighten out the circle. The room was filled with anticipation. Although Pat Howard had poked her head into the classroom often that year, it wasn't until this June morning that she paid her first official visit.

To the children's delight, Mrs. Howard once again went through the ritual of holding her hip and sighing loudly as she climbed down onto the floor with the children. "You've even got Mrs. Currier sitting on the floor," she said, winking at Carolyn. "I don't believe you guys."

When the room quieted, Mrs. Currier said, "In honor of Mrs. Howard's visit, let's just go around the circle and each of you can tell us where you are in the writing process." Then she said to Diane, "Diane, what are you working on?"

Diane was writing a letter to her friend. Amy said she *might* be starting a poem. Craig was making a hardcover book to hold his final drafts from the year. "It's even going to have a Table of Contents and About the Author and that stuff," he said.

Vin had finished his whale report and needed a conference. Birger announced that he and Alan and Jeremy had a secret project in the library. Then he added, "It has to do with leads."

Susie had given up on her make-believe story and was writing what she described as "sort of a book report, only not so boring." Eric didn't know what he was doing, but he pretended it was a secret. And the list of projects and plans continued.

When the meeting was over, the children dispersed. For a few minutes, Carolyn, Pat and I sat on the carpet. The clatter of transition subsided into a workshop hum. We surveyed the room, noticing that the children had all settled into their work. "I guess they don't need me anymore," Carolyn joked, unaware that there was truth in her observation.

Carolyn and Pat began to get up, but I told them to wait. For a few minutes I rummaged about the classroom, returning with two clipboards. "Why don't you help me take notes," I said, "the kids don't need any help." And so the three of us began moving about the classroom, watching and documenting what the children were doing.

Amy had indeed begun a poem. "I had it in my mind so it was easy to write," she said and showed us a draft titled "Markings." "It's messy," she warned. . .

I jerk ^{marking} my pencil,
it makes a ~~rough~~ line.

Lightly I run it,
It makes a delicate line
I never lift it of the paper,
It makes a flowing line.

It quivers

On the ^{lovely} face of a beautiful
girl

Across the table from Amy, Diane bent low over her work. We could not see the paper, her arm shielded it from us. We knew she was writing a letter and so I asked, "Is it private?"

"Well, sort of," Diane said, "but after watching me for two years, you already know my personal things, you and Susie." I drew my chair closer, and Diane slid her paper toward me. I read it silently, then Diane said, "They can see it too," and so Carolyn and Pat drew into our circle. None of us said anything as we read what Diane had written, but Diane knew we understood.

Dear Jessie,
"Hi, How are you?" "I'm fine." Why haven't you been writing back to me? I've always said on the bottom of the letters that I

sent you "Write back Soon", but you never do. I miss you more than you'd ever imagine. Whenever you come up to N.H., & when we have the big 4th of July party, you never play with me. It's always Holly or Sarah but never me. Don't you like me anymore? I know that I'm not to exciting when it comes to playing but when you avoid me... I feel like I just lost my dearest friend. This years 4th of July party, will you play with me? Or am I too boring? Truthfully, am I boring? I would feel very good if you played with me this years party. Hey Jess, do you think that when you & your family come up to N.H., for the weeked, would you like to stay at our house? Your family & all? We'd love to have you stay over for the whole weekend.

A while back, do you remember when my mother called your mother? Well, you didn't sound thrilled to talk to me, did you not feel good or something? Truthfully, am I still your best friend?

Do you like my school picture? I hate it. I look terrible in it. Talking about school pictures, I just went over to Charlies' house and saw your school picture. You now, you're really pretty with your hair up, in braids and in a bun. You look very different from when we came down. We might be coming down this April vaca-

_tion. I want to very, very, much. Well, I have to go now, bye, best friend!

_____ (I think) Your best friend,
                         Diane

As we moved on, Pat asked about Diane. Had her writing gotten better this year? Did she and Susie still play together at home? Did they still do their pretend games—like throwing birdseed in each other's hair and make-believing the seeds were a veil and they were brides . . .

We reached the table where Susie was reading her book report to Trish.

What do you do on a rainy Saturday? That's what the Melendy children wanted to know. There wasn't anything to do. The Melendy children are: Mandy, Miranda, and Oliver. Then they got a wonderful idea. They would make Saturdays better days. They would donate their allowance to one of the kids. Then that person goes somewhere that interests him. They would do that until everbody got a turn . . .

When Susie finished reading, Trish said, "I like it but there is one thing—it sounds like you are following right along with the book, not skipping."

Susie looked down at the book report. "Yeah, and I'm not too pleased with where I explain what the plan is," she said. "I could have them giving the plan to Miranda. I might try that. I'll still start 'What do you do on a rainy Saturday' but then whoever got the plan, I'll say 'So and so got an idea!'"

Susie began writing the second draft of her book report:

What do you do on a rainy Saturday? That's what the Melendy children wanted to know.

The children sulked around their playroom on this rainy day. "I've got an idea for something we can do . . . "

Meanwhile, Birger's secret project turned out not to be so secret. In fact, he came back from the library asking whether Mrs. Howard had forgotten where he was working. We took the hint and were glad of it. The boys had recruited the librarian's help and the four of them were going through books in search of good leads. Birger explained, "When I found out my leads were a disaster, I decided to see how other people do it, how they start off." Birger added, "We're going to write down all the good leads and then read them to the other kids."

Back in the classroom, the children continued their work. Several were at the editing table using dictionaries or Roget's Thesaurus. "I went through my writing, circling all the little words and I'm going to change them to bigger ones," Jeremy told us.

Craig was on the carpet, his finished book in hand. "I'm waiting for share meeting," he told us, "my book is all done!"

"Would you show it to us?" we asked, climbing onto the floor beside Craig, who made no effort to conceal his delight.

"Here's my first story, I wrote like a baby back then," he said and quickly turned to the next page. Page by page, we followed Craig's progress.

"Amazing how someone could change so much," Pat said, and Carolyn nodded.

I looked at the two of them, sitting close to Craig, studying the progress in his drafts. "Amazing," I agreed.

Bibliography

Agar, M. *The Professional Stranger*. New York: Harcourt Brace Jovanovich, 1980.

Bereiter, C. "From Conversation to Composition: The Role of Instruction in a Developmental Process." In R. Glaser (ed.) *Advances in Instructional Psychology* (vol. 2). Hillsdale, New Jersey: Erlbaum, in press.

Bruner, J. *The Process of Education*. New York: Random House, 1963.

Bruner, J. *Toward a Theory of Instruction*. Cambridge, Massachusetts: Harvard University Press, 1966.

Calkins, L. "Children's Rewriting Strategies," *Research in the Teaching of English*. January, 1981.

Cazden, C. *Child Language and Education*. New York: Holt, Rinehart and Winston, 1972.

Donaldson, M. *Children's Minds*. New York: Norton and Co., 1978.

Elbow, P. *Writing with Power*. New York: Oxford University Press, 1981.

Flower, L. and Hayes, J.R. "The Dynamics of Composing: Making Plans and Juggling Constraints." In *Cognitive Processes in Writing: An Interdisciplinary Approach*. Eds. Gregg and Steinberg. Hillsdale, New Jersey: Erlbaum, 1980.

Flower, L. and Hayes, J.R. "Plans that Guide the Composing Process," In *Writing: The Nature, Development and Teaching of Written Composition*. Eds. Frederikson and Dominic. Hillsdale, New Jersey: Erlbaum, 1981.

Gardner, H. *Artful Scribbles*. New York: Basic Books, 1980.

Graves, D. *Writing: Teachers and Children at Work*. Exeter, New Hampshire: Heinemann, 1983.

Kelly, G. *A Theory of Personality*. New York: Norton and Co., 1963.

Murray, D. *A Writer Teaches Writing*. Boston, Massachusetts: Houghton Mifflin, 1968.

Murray, D. "The Listening Eye," *College English*. September, 1979.

Newkirk, T. "Young Writers as Critical Readers," *Language Arts*, 1982.

Perl, S. Five Writers Writing: The Composing Processes of Five Unskilled College Writers. Doctoral dissertation, New York University, 1978.

Perl, S. "Unskilled Writers as Composers," *New York Education Quarterly*, **10**, 1979.

Vygotsky, L. *Thought and Language.* Cambridge, Massachusetts: M.I.T. Press, 1962.

Zinsser, W. *On Writing Well.* New York: Harper and Row.

Index

Action, 66, 67, 77, 107, 120
Amy, 20, 43, 67, 70, 89, 108, 109, 133; and peer conferences, 122−123, 128; planning for writing by, 31; poetry by, 172, 173; report writing by, 165−166; writing of, 16, 108−109
Arrows, as revision code, 44, 46−47, 59
Atkinson Elementary School, 3, 6, 7, 9, 68, 76, 161
Audience, 65−67; concept development and, 145; internalizing, 18−19, 58−61, 139−140; peer pressure from, 60; revising out of concern for, 49, 69, 70, 72, 139, 140, 154−155; need to trust, 115

Beginning Writing Workshop, 26
Bereiter, Carl, 57−58, 60
Birger, 17, 20, 70, 135; sound effects and exclamation marks, 56−57; and peer conferences, 120, 122−124; and punctuation, 35; and reading-writing connection, 157, 160; report writing by, 165; secret project of, 172, 175; voting box of,118; writing of, 3, 95, 115, 133−134, 153

Brainstorming, 118
Bruner, J., 50, 63−64, 136; *A Theory of Instruction*, 57
Byars, Betsy, *The Midnight Fox*, 77

Case study, 3, 5, 7, 8, 10
Circle-and-expand strategy, 93−95, 97, 99
Clarity, revising out of concern for, 49,141, 154−155
Classroom: materials for, 13, 27−28, 110; organization of, 30−32, 70, 109−110, 116
Cognitive development, 50−54, 57−58, 62
Colon, 34
Commas, 36
Concept development, 65−67, 142−151
Conferences
peer, 60, 61, 68−99, 109, 110, 114, 131, 134, 165, 166; teacher: child, 35−40, 44−46, 131−137; researcher: child, 136−137; with oneself, 4, 138−141; response group, 97, 111

content of, 132−134; process, 45−46, 93, 134−136; evaluation, 137; editing, 34

in classroom organization,

39; learning to confer, 38–40; questions, 126, 129–130, 134

Content area writing, *See* reports

Convention, 66; concern for, 4, 10, 13, 14

Craig, 39, 70, 127, 135, 136; and editing, 23, 34, 36; hardcover book made by, 172, 176; and reading-writing connection, 160; report writing by, 165, 166; and topic choice, 27; writing of, 17, 21, 36, 106–107, 115, 116

Currier, Carolyn, 22, 76, 90, 101, 105–106; her approach to teaching writing, 109–111, 114–116; and large-scale revisions by Susie, 93, 95; and peer conferences, 114–121; and reading-writing connection, 158–159; and report writing, 161, 162, 164, 165, 166; and teacher:child conferences, 131–137; teacher collaboration on new ideas by, 105–113; teaching children to teach each other by, 125–130; variety in work of students of, 172–176; and writers' circle, 97

Data collection, 9, 10, 16, 17, 20–22, 55

Detail, 66, 67, 78; writing with, 56

Dialogue: leads involving, 77; writing with, 56, 57, 122, 123

Diane, 4, 16–17, 24, 26, 39,

70; and conference with oneself, 138; dialogue used by, 56, 57; on drafts, 135; and glacier report by Susie, 164; letter writing by, 172, 173–175; and peer conferences, 117–123, 125; and reading-writing connection, 154, 160; report writing by, 165, 166; and structure of writing workshop, 30; and Susie's writing, 43, 58, 59, 60, 71, 99, 140–141; and topic choice, 27, 117–119; writing of, 73, 107–108, 115

Dividing line strategy, 90, 95, 97

Donaldson, M., 132, 136

Dry periods, 20, 21, 29. *See also* Writer's block

Editing, 33–36, 56, 57, 116; area for, in classroom, 109; checklists, 33–34; children with problems in, 20–23, 34, 36, 106, 107, 116; conferences, 34; growth in, 34–36, 106, 107; peer, 34

Elbow, Peter, *Writing with Power*, 97, 111

Endings, 10, 66, 149–150, 158

Exclamation marks, 56, 57, 121

Executive function, 55–61, 67, 160, 163

Fiction, 145, 172

Field of concerns, expanding dimensions of, 55, 65–67

First graders, 11, 12, 13, 49, 50, 67, 121, 139, 154, 155, 157

Flashbacks, 77
Flower, L., 58, 64, 65, 147, 151
Focus, 65–67, 77, 78, 133, 143, 148, 149, 153
Fourth grade, 82–90, 172–176

Gardner, Howard, 18, 142, 143
Giacobbe, Mary Ellen, 11, 37, 67, 121, 137; approach of, to early writing, 12, 13; conferences of, 131, 132; publishing by first graders of, 110; revision by first graders of, 49, 50
Glacier report, Susie's, 161, 162–164, 166, 167–171
Graves, Donald, 9–10, 12, 22; and concept development, 142; on good writing classroom, 27; and N.I.E. study, 5–7, 13, 23; on reading-writing connection, 152, 160; and structure of writing workshop, 30; and topic choice, 25

Hayes, J.R., 58, 64, 65
Howard, Pat, 9, 11, 14–17, 20, 101; approach of, to teaching writing, 14–16, 18, 22–23, 37–40; classroom of, 9, 13–14, 30–32; conferences of, 39–40, 58, 131; and editing, 33–35; interventions of, in Susie's writing, 43–48; mini-lessons of, 76, 77–78; and peer conferences, 121; and qualities of good writing, 67; and revision by

third graders, 49, 51; role of, as teacher, 37–40; and share meetings, 126; on sharing work-in-process, 60; on Sible family, 21; and structure of writing workshop, 30–32, 114; and Susie's snuggling story, 68–75; teacher collaboration on new ideas by, 105–113; and topic choice, 24–28; variety in work of former students of, 172–176; her work on focus, 77

Internalization of concrete physical strategies 55, 62–65, 67, 71, 80–84, 100
Interviews, 26–27
Invented spelling, 11–13, 38

Leads, 77, 78, 79, 158, 166–167; peer conferences on, 120
Lead-writing strategy, 45–47, 52–53, 63, 64, 71–73, 87, 98–99
Letter writing, 116, 173–175
Literature, 109; to illustrate good leads, 77

Mapping, 77–78, 163
Mini-lessons, 31, 76, 109, 162; on mapping, 77–78; on note taking, 162; on revision strategies, 95; use of, to teach skills of peer conferencing, 125–130
Murray, Donald M., 28, 39, 139, 150; *A Writer Teaches Writing*, 78

Narratives, personal, 24–29, 76–77, 112, 145
National Institute of Education (NIE), 5, 6, 23, 131, 132
New Hampshire, University of, 5–6, 28, 39, 68, 146
Newkirk, T., 67, 156–157

Organization, 66, 77, 78, 99–100, 163
Outlining, see Mapping
Ownership, 23, 131

Pace, 14, 30–32, 109, 116
Paragraphing, 34
Peer conferences, see Conferences
Penmanship, changes in, 89–90
Pen pal, see Letter writing
Perl, Sondra, 61
Piaget, Jean, 62, 136
Plot, 158
Poetic license, 148, 149
Poetry, 140–141, 173
Point-of-view, 158
Publishing, 109–112
Punctuation, 10n; teaching, 33–36, 56–67

Qualities of good writing, 65–67, 128, 143; action, 66–67, 146; information, 24, 28, 66; organization, 77–78, 99–100, 163; showing, 78, 108, 122, 123; truth, 147
Quotation marks, 34–35

Reading: 152–171; and asking questions, 160–161; conferences, 158–159; connection between writing and, 152–159, 163; imbalance between basics of writing and, 152–153; as process, 153; skills learned through writing, 153
Report writing, 3, 116, 119, 161–171
Research, background to N.I.E., 5–8; data collection, 9, 10, 16, 17, 20–22; influence on teaching, 14, 15, 22–23, 37–40, 135, 137; purpose, 3, 4, 7; teacher's role, 14–16; team members, 7, See also conferences
Retelling, 147, 148
Revision: anticipating more drafts, 47, 50; changes in third and fourth grades, 64–65, 76–88, 98–99; cognitive development and, 50, 57–58; development of executive function in, 55–61; differences in drafts in, 3, 4, 52, 53, 58–59, 71–74, 92–98, 108, 109, 168–171; drafts malleable, 44–48, 50, 59, 74, 90–101; early forms, 43–48, 51–54, 56–61; by first graders, 49–50, 139; importance to revise, 47, 49, 50–51, 71, 79, 85–86; incongruities leading to, 47; inventing new strategies, 63, 82, 90–101; large scale in fourth grade, 90–101

See also circle-and-expand strategy, concept development, internalization, leads

Rules, importance of, 31, 32, 70

Schedule, 14, 30–32, 121
Sequence, 66, 67; developing reading skill of, 154
Share meetings, 3, 4, 31, 68–69, 72, 111, 115, 126–130, 165
Sharing writing, 31, 60, 68, 72, 109, 112
Sible family, 21
Site selection, 67
Smith, Frank, 133, 139
Sound effects, 67; overuse of, 56, 57
Sowers, Susan, 7, 13, 22
Spelling, 10n, 21, 22, 33, *See also* Craig
Susie, 21, 25, 136; book report of, 172, 175; changes in revision by, between third and fourth grades, 76–88; changes in writing of, 23, 40, 43–48; concept development of, 142–151; and conference with oneself, 138, 140–141; development of executive function by, 55–61; dimensions of her fields of concern, 55, 65–67; her friendship with Diane, 16, 26; glacier report of, 161, 162–164, 166, 167–171; growth of, 7, 19; influence of, on classmates, 26–27; internalizing concrete physical strategies by, 55, 62–65, 67; large-scale revisions of, 90–101; lead-writing strategy of, 63, 64–65; learning good peer conference questions by, 125–126, 127, 129; peer conferences of, 117–124; penmanship of, 89–90; and reading-writing connection, 152, 153, 157–158, 160, 163; revision by, 49–54; snuggling story of, 68–75; and structure of writing workshop, 30, 31; topic choice by, 62–63, 64; writing of, 3–5, 10, 12, 13, 17–19; as writing teacher, 114

Teacher, role: changes in, 37–40; in conferences, 35–40, 44–46, 131–137; in classroom organization, 30–32, 39; in editing, 33–36; in peer conferences, 125–128; in research, 14–16, 20–23, 38–39
Third grade conventionality, 10, 12, 13, 14, 18–19, 33; characteristics of text, 56–57; revision, 49–64
Time/space frames, 54, 85, 87
Tone, 66
Topic(s): assigned versus chosen, 24–29, 62–63, 64, 76–77, 117–119; focus, 45; helping children find, 25–29, 138
Truth, 66; concern for, 144, 146–148

Voice, 11, 12, 165, 166
Vygotsky, L., 60, 136

Whole-class meetings, *see* Share meetings
Writer's block, 20, 29, 117, 119. *See also* Dry periods

Writers' circle, 97, 111. *see* response groups
Writing folders, 29, 70; cumulative, 73, 106, 110; daily, 73, 110

Writing workshop, *see* classroom organization, beginning writing workshops